Praise for
Loss Is a Four-Letter Word

"Carole Brody Fleet is forthright in dealing with many of the difficult issues surrounding widowhood, demonstrating that you do   have to live in your past. It's not an either-or situation. She teach   tant lesson that you can incorporate your previous life in

—**Jane Brod**

"Carole Brody Fleet has done it ɛ   er Word, she offers practical, straightforward a   forward on a positive path after losing a loved one. ɪ   ɑs a guest on the *Angel Quest* radio show a number of times   of how much she has benefited my listeners with her knowledge. If ɪɩ ɔounds like I am impressed with her, it's because I am. I love this book, and I love Carole!"

—**Karen Noé**, author, *We Consciousness: 33 Profound Truths for Inner and Outer Peace* and *Your Life After Their Death: A Medium's Guide to Healing After a Loss*

"Just as there is no timetable for grief, there certainly is no checklist on how to recover strength and joy after suffering a loss. Here you will find authentic, candid, trustworthy, and—perhaps most pertinent of all—pragmatic advice promising that, although the landscape of life may forever be changed, the future can still hold purpose, beauty, and magic. With a signature style all her own, Carole Brody Fleet "trains" you to find yourself again (hint: there's no wrong path, but some are healthier for your soul!). Together, you will navigate everything from social media to financial matters to the possibility of finding love again. Sure, it can feel impossible to do, and even more so to find answers, but sign up, dear recruit, and discover this book's wit and wisdom, and its author's enormous-as-the-universe heart!"

—**Kristin Higson-Hughes**, senior features editor, *Woman's World* magazine

"What I love and appreciate is Carole Brody Fleet's firsthand knowledge and approach on the most taboo topic in society. Having gone through personal loss, I always learn something about how to approach the topic with empathy and how to permit others to comfort me in the worst of times."

—**Lisa Lockwood**, crime analyst, author, police and military veteran

"Carole Brody Fleet is the real deal. In her latest act of service, *Loss Is a Four-Letter Word*, Carole helps the widowed navigate the unknown waters of loss and grief. She does not write or speak from a lofty position but instead from her heart, mind, and soul. She has a personal stake because she, too, has experienced the loss of her husband. In the multiple radio program conversations I've had with her, Carole has been articulate, savvy, graceful, and funny, yet she has displayed deep compassion for those who are suffering. This is a book that you can give to a family member, friend, or office associate and know that you've selected one of the best there is to help the person find themselves after loss. There *is* hope, and Carole Brody Fleet embodies that in her compassionate work with those who, like herself, have experienced the long dark night of the soul. She pulls no punches and I appreciate her all the more for doing so. Read this book!"

—**Scott H. Colborn,** host, KZUM FM's,
Exploring Unexplained Phenomena radio show

"Carole Brody Fleet has faced painful challenges and loss with courage and resilience. Through her own personal healing, we can all learn from and be inspired by her. I have a four-letter word for Carole: HERO."

—**Stacey Gualandi,**
Emmy Award-winning journalist

"Carole is an angel, not just an expert. Many of us have no clue what to say to a loved one going through tremendous loss. We sit by and watch helplessly as they struggle with their "new normal." Carole's book is a must read, not just for widows but for those of us who love a widow as well. As a relationship radio talk-show host, I have always had words to comfort and guide someone through every type of heartache—every heartache except the death of a spouse. This type of loss leaves many of us speechless. Finally, someone who knows what to say when the rest of us do not."

—**Kim Iversen,**
nationally syndicated radio show host

LOSS Is a FOUR-LETTER WORD

A BEREAVEMENT BOOT CAMP FOR THE WIDOWED

Kick Grief in the Ass and Take Your Life Back

Carole Brody Fleet

Health Communications, Inc.
Deerfield Beach, Florida

www.hcibooks.com

**Library of Congress Cataloging-in-Publication Data
is available through the Library of Congress**

© 2018 Carole Brody Fleet

ISBN-13: 978-07573-2121-4 (Paperback)
ISBN-10: 07573-2121-6 (Paperback)
ISBN-13: 978-07573-2122-1 (ePub)
ISBN-10: 07573-2122-4 (ePub)

Publisher: Health Communications, Inc.
    3201 S.W. 15th Street
    Deerfield Beach, FL 33442–8190

Cover and interior design and formatting by Lawna Patterson Oldfield

This book is lovingly dedicated to:

All those who comprise the widowed community today
and to those who will one day join this community:
May your healing journey be enhanced and enriched, and may your
heart and spirit be lifted as you pursue your healing journeys.

Eilene Clinkenbeard
For continuing to believe in your crazy, writer-chick daughter
and for always allowing me to share your inimitable Mom-isms. *Aloha nui loa.*

Kendall Leah Brody, Michelle Louise Stansbury, and Natasha Tillett Slayton:
You are now and forever the true beauties, the
bright lights, and the loves of my life.
Mommy loves you so much.

Dave Stansbury
To my partner in life and in love: Thank you for putting up with more
"take-out" than "home-cooked"; for reminding me each day
to chase the dream, and the "just for fun" that is us.
I love you very much.

Elvin "Clink" Clinkenbeard (1923–2001) and Michael Fleet, Sr. (1945–2000)
You continue to give me strength every day as my work
continues to be to your honor.
I love you both without end.

Teddie Tillett (1953–2016)
While the hole you left in our hearts will never completely heal,
we are comforted by the legacies of love and laughter
that you have left to each one of us.

I love you forever.

Contents

Acknowledgments

I gratefully acknowledge those who have supported this project with their time, wisdom, patience, and love.

Nothing happens without there first being a team of visionaries. I am incredibly blessed to work with the creative visionaries that comprise HCI Books; including the amazing Christine Belleris, Kim Weiss, Ian Briggs, Lawna Oldfield, Mary Ellen Hettinger, and the entire HCI team, who are each committed to both the vision of their authors and the betterment of people's lives.

My "Glam Squad" remains second to none, and I would be lost without Ashley Whitcomb, Brandon Hyman, Pamela Marches, and Alex and everyone on the "Happy Team." Thank you all for putting up with me, my last-minute nonsense, and for seeing to it that everything happens when and as needed.

I am so fortunate to have worked with an incredible group of people who are always ready and willing to help reach an audience in need. I give my sincerest thanks and deepest gratitude to the many members of the media in the United States, Canada, and in the United Kingdom with whom I have the privilege of working, for all of your support in delivering the messages of hope to the millions who need to hear it. My thanks and gratitude also to my "families" at *Chicken Soup for the Soul, The Huffington Post* and *ThirdAge.com.*

I have always said that out of tragedy, blessings can emerge in the form of earth angels. My earth angels include Kristen Higson-Hughes, Lee and Bob Woodruff, Jennifer Arches, Stacey Gualandi, Shannon Bell, Karen Noé, Kathleen Martin, Scott Colburn, James Patrick Herman, and Christopher Bahls. Thank you all for being the earth angels in my life.

When the people of your long-ago choose to support your present, it must be celebrated and appreciated. I lovingly celebrate this moment with: Karen (Anderson) Cooper, Laura (Billingsley) Evink, Susan (Venuti) Hampton, Lisa Guest, Taryn Whiteleather, Kathy (Green) Schutt, Nancy (Lum) Korb, Pamela (Jaques) Marches, Karen (Ingram) Sanchez, Dave and Guyla (Wilkerson) Romero, Dr. Carla Payne (Beach Boys forever!), Tracy Jones, Dr. Mark Ivanicki, Gary and Elissa Wahlenmaier, Mercy Songcayauon Cheung, Rosie "Bing Bing" Gasche, Mariellen Belen, Lyn Ramirez, Royce Ramirez, Rachelle Basso and Rhonda Okurowski, Linda (Snyder) Steward (greatest roommate *ever!*), my most precious Shellee (Brown) and Bob Renaud, and the inimitable Debra Boyd (*still* waiting on the mezzanine for chicken enchiladas). Your continued love and support mean everything to me.

Bobby Slayton, through the very worst and the very best of times, you never fail to be there for me and for my family. It is with love that I thank you for continuing to remind all of us that it will always be okay to laugh; no matter what life throws at us.

Without my family, there is no success, and it is with all my love that I thank my Dave "Stanno" Stansbury; my amazing daughters,

Kendall ("OG Daughter"), Michelle ("English Daughter"), and Natasha ("Bonus/Angel Daughter") and the "Leader of the Team," my mother, Eilene Clinkenbeard; as well as my "Son I Didn't Need to Get Stretch Marks to Have," David Johnston, and my "Triple A Kittens," Aubrey Johnston, Ainsley Johnston, and Amelie Johnston; Kenneth "The Boss" Stansbury (of blessed memory); Terry and Pam Stansbury and the Leeson/Gullick Families; Jen and Gloria Bulger, David Clinkenbeard; Russell Gilbert, MD, and Kiyomi Gilbert; Linda Ciampoli; Max Ciampoli (of blessed memory); the dynamic duo of Chuck Collins and Randy George; and every single member of the Berman/Spielman/Horn Families; the Williamson Families; the Zimmer Family and the Bobinsky/Fahrenkrug/Borg Families.

Finally, to my sister of the soul, Teddie "Turtle" Tillett Slayton (12/28/53–3/23/16): As you soar with the angels, you will forever remain my "sister," my heart, and my center of gravity. I love you. Macaroni.

Prologue

What do you think is the first image that enters the mind of most people when they hear the word "widowed"? If referring to a widowed woman, chances are that the image is of someone in her golden years, who is perennially dressed in black, plays a lot of bingo, and has difficulty walking. Similarly, a widower is also thought of as one who is somewhat older, has the same difficulty walking, and begins searching desperately for a new wife approximately twenty minutes after his beloved has passed away.

Even though stereotypes exist because on some level, they are based in a rare reality, the fact is that the image of the widowed must be broadened dramatically. How do I know? Because along with millions of others in the widowed community, I too have heard the following phrases too many times to count:

"No one lives forever."

"How can *you* be widowed?"

"You're too young to be a widow."

As well as the converse:

"I would expect someone *your* age to be widowed."
"You're a widow? Stay away from me!" (usually said while making
   a cross with two fingers).
"You're widowed? You sure don't look/act like it."

After years of listening to phrases like these (and many more
like them), I asked myself at long last: *What* does *widowed really
look like?* In my continuing quest to break the stereotype of how
the widowed are viewed, allow me to introduce you to this wonderful community as entirely and as all-inclusively as is possible:

We are *not* the image of widowed that the world purports us
to be.

No widowed look exactly the same.

No widow*hood* looks exactly the same.

Therefore, no healing journey or timeline is exactly the same.

Widowhood does not discriminate and is arbitrary in its attack.

There is no "minimum age requirement" involved with widowhood.

We come from both genders, in *all* age groups, and from *all* walks
   of life.

We are opposite-sex spouses and we are same-sex spouses.

Our beloveds were lost suddenly and without warning.

Our beloveds died after suffering the ravages of long-term illness
   or infirmity for months or even years.

We were engaged to be married, and death stole our beloved
   away before we had the opportunity to walk down an aisle.

We were in long-term relationships that people around us easily trivialize or dismiss altogether; stating that it should be

"easier" for us to get over the death of our beloveds because we "weren't really a couple."

We were married for many decades.

We were married for a few years.

We were married for mere months . . . or days . . . or hours.

We have adult children.

We have young children.

We were left pregnant.

We never had the chance to have children at all.

We are retired.

We are still in the workplace and must return to work in the midst of grieving.

We are faced with returning to the workplace after staying at home with our children and are unsure of our place in a professional world.

We are faced with a life that we are not sure how to live.

We likely know no one to talk to who really understands.

We have questions about this new life that we have been handed; questions that we want to ask so badly, but are afraid of what other people may say or think if we dare.

We wear black because it is a fashion statement; not because we are in perpetual mourning.

We celebrate when we accomplish something new; whether it is fixing something in the house or going out for a meal on our own.

We wish that people were not afraid of us.

We wish that you would call.

We wish that you would mention their name.

We cry when no one is watching.

We also laugh because it feels *so* good to do so once again . . . but laughing again does not mean that we have forgotten who and what we have lost.

We take baby steps into a life for which we did not enroll; yet are left behind to live.

We want to live fully again and are not sure how to go about doing so.

We are derided (and worse) by those whom we once trusted and believed would always be a source of support for us and for our children.

We are also loved and supported by incredibly special people in our lives without whom our healing journeys would be impossibly empty and we would be otherwise hopelessly lost.

We do not want to be looked at peculiarly.

We do not want to be treated as though we carry a contagious disease called Death.

We do not want pity.

We simply want help without reproach.

We want education without lecture.

We want support without judgment, condition, or negative opinion.

Because . . . while our spouses may have departed this earth, we are still here.

And we matter too.

Introduction

*L*oss. A word containing only four letters, yet it is so enormous in scope that it has the capacity to strike terror into hearts everywhere. Even more terrifying is the reality of loss, specifically, the loss of a spouse. I know that terror. I know that reality. I *did* that loss.

After a lengthy, highly decorated and award-winning career as a police officer, my husband Mike retired from his department, only to be diagnosed with ALS (amyotrophic lateral sclerosis, commonly known as Lou Gehrig's disease) two weeks later. With that diagnosis arrived a devastating new reality, that in the not-too-distant future, our then nine-year-old daughter Kendall and I were going to be alone.

With more strength, grace, and dignity than one could possibly imagine, Mike courageously battled his illness with every bit of strength in his very being. Three years after the first symptoms appeared and two years after his diagnosis, the end came peacefully, at home, as was Mike's wish.[1]

Mike's was an extremely large funeral. The funeral director remarked that it was the second-largest funeral that their company had ever handled. Law enforcement officers of varying ranks and representing police departments throughout several states were in

---

1 Actually, it was more like a demand.

attendance, as well as officials from all manner of state and federal government agencies. It was a day rich in remembrance, tradition, and honor—simultaneously fraught with what I can only describe as a hazy, surreal mélange of overwhelming grief and Novocain-like numbness, occasionally punctuated by mental snapshots of one of the worst days that I will ever endure.

Then the next morning came . . . and what everyone was referring to as my "new normal" had unceremoniously begun.[2]

The loss of a spouse is frightening. It brings us to our knees. It leaves us feeling rudderless—and the ensuing grief can be all-consuming and seemingly never-ending. Regardless of the circumstances, spousal loss devastates on numerous levels and in countless ways. Whether the loss is brand new or decades old, it nonetheless cuts, wounds, and scars. Worst of all, and if we permit it to do so, widowhood can also be capable of keeping us from moving forward into a new life filled with abundance, and peace, and all of the wonderful things that life offers to us on a daily basis.

Personally, I flat-out refused.

I refused to be defined by a set of circumstances that would have otherwise kept me in mourning for the rest of my life, not to mention the irreparable harm that permanent residence in said mourning place would have caused to my adolescent daughter. I refused to stay inside, alone and sobbing in the dark for the rest of my days. I refused to allow the disease that stole my husband from his family and our future to claim our lives as well.

Instead, I made a conscious decision. I decided that everlasting mourning was a false destiny; a destiny that I did not choose—and

2 I *hate* that phrase. Think about it . . . have you ever noticed that no one *ever* uses the phrase, "new normal" in reference to anything positive? No one ever wins a lottery and yells, *"This is my new normal!"*

if I do not choose something, it generally means that I do not want it. I decided to both embark upon and model a grief recovery that, while not without a few hiccups, was going to be healthy and productive. I decided that I would take back control of a life over which I'd had little control since the evil of illness invaded and commandeered our lives.

I decided that even though my future was not going to be the one that we had originally planned, I am nevertheless still the architect who can design and frame and couch and inform the future that I wish for both myself and my daughter.

In other words, I decided to kick grief right in its great big ugly ass.

How?

By refusing to live a life any less than what *any* of us deserve to live—and that includes *you*.

Welcome to Bereavement Boot Camp (and a Whole Lot More)

This book combines no-nonsense, straightforward, and occasionally tough-talking practical advice with Bereavement Boot Camp, complete with assignments that are designed to help you move forward from (*not* "get over") a most profound loss in positive ways. Appropriate for both the newly widowed as well as for those of you who may have been grieving for years, and regardless of age, gender, technical marital status, or sexual orientation, this book is also ideal for those of you who know and love someone who is widowed, and who wants to learn how to best support them through this, one of the most challenging life journeys of them all.

In addition to Bereavement Boot Camp lessons and assignments, you will find chapters designed to provide you with added insight, education, motivation, support, answers to your many questions, and perhaps even a smile or two along the way. You may occasionally recognize advice that you have seen or heard from me before and with good reason. It is valuable advice that bears repeating and advice that everyone needs to either learn initially or hear again (and again . . . and *again*).

Just as with the Boot Camp lessons, some of the ancillary chapters may be tough to read, perhaps even potentially controversial. While I do not intentionally seek to be controversial (which is explained in-depth a little later on), I also refuse to shy away from the traditionally difficult subjects and challenges that surround widowhood. The reasoning is simple. Imagine the widow who believes that she is the only one in the world who feels a sense of relief that her spouse is gone, or the reader who is destructively coping with their grief and feels helpless to stop. Envision the readers who think that they are alone in their challenges as they try to deal with the things that people are saying, or the readers who have been abandoned by those whom they once trusted.

We are going to discuss all of those subjects—and a whole lot more.

Sarah Silverman, a brilliant comedienne, said it best when she stated, "If I'm not willing to be controversial, what am I doing here?" I precisely echo her sentiment. My goal is to get every single reader on a positive path to healing after loss and, in so doing, I am both delighted and happily willing to embrace the tough, the controversial, the uncomfortable, and the sweep-it-under-the-carpet topics and issues.

One of the biggest assets that I am also happy to provide is a list of resources for you to consult and explore. From organizations that specifically work with and support the widowed community, to multiple organizations who can help you (or someone you love) cope with a wide variety of difficulties that face our community, there is help readily available to you. You will find the list of Recommended Resources in the back of the book.

In and amongst all of this information you're going to find what I call an "Extra Kick In The Ass" (**EKITA!**) if you will—because let's face it, we all need a few of those EKITAs in order to keep focused along our healing journeys, especially on the challenging days. Most importantly, you are going to quickly discover that you are not alone in your feelings and experiences, which is the first and most vital avenue of comfort that I can offer.

Yes, loss *is* indeed a four-letter word. However, it is also within our power to ensure that our losses are experiences that will shape us, and not labels that will define us. Let's now begin our work together—and kick grief in the ass!

Bereavement Boot Camp Lesson One: I'm Still Here

D o you right now feel stuck in a place of loss? Do you feel as though you have at all begun your healing journey in earnest? Do you feel as though the way you feel right now, today, is the way that you will feel forever? Do you not know how to answer any of these questions? Welcome to Lesson One of Bereavement Boot Camp.

Did I just scare you? *Relax.* Let me first reassure you that Bereavement Boot Camp does not include barking drill sergeants and twenty-mile hikes. What it *does* involve is *you* getting serious with and about *you* and *your* healing. It involves *you* committing to *you* that *you* are going to do one tiny thing every single day to move *yourself* out of a place of pain and move forward toward a place of peace.

Did you note the repeated emphases on the words, *"you"* and *"your"*? There is a really good reason for that emphasis: you may have not put any real emphasis on yourself for a very long time. Guess what? The time to put yourself at the top of your own to-do list has just arrived.

Getting serious with yourself and choosing to either begin or move forward on a healing journey sounds pretty obvious, doesn't it? Perhaps—but it might surprise you to learn just how many people choose against either starting or continuing forward from a place of grief to a place of peace. While there is certainly no argument that grieving your loss is essential, so too is healing . . . and your healing process begins (or continues) right now.

Each Boot Camp chapter is based upon an affirmation borne of my own loss experience. These chapters and affirmations are specifically designed to help you move through whatever obstacles might be holding you back from reaching the destiny that *you* choose to design and that *you* deserve. Take each affirmation (or EKITA) and put it in a place where you will see it every day, the more often the better. Start your day and end your day with an affirmation or an EKITA. Why? It's a very simple bereavement recovery math equation: Affirmation equals reinforcement; reinforcement creates belief; belief creates proactivity, and proactivity is the foundation of healing.

You may be thinking to yourself, *So, Carole, I go through the Boot Camp and read all of the other chapters and EKITAs and immerse myself in affirmations and complete all of the Boot Camp assignments. Does that mean that by the end of the book, the grief and pain will be totally gone?* Of course not. I personally get pretty riled up when I see other grief recovery books (or programs, CDs, webinars, seminars, and the like) make claims like "Feel Better in No Time" or "Grief Be Gone in X Amount of Days." Claims such as these are akin to ads that attempt to entice us with "Lose Forty Pounds in Thirty Days." It is not only false advertising, it is both an impossible and unattainable goal—and when you do not feel better within the promised amount of time, you feel even worse for failing to attain the unattainable.

My core belief has always been that no one can guarantee emotional healing of any kind within any set period of time (especially if the word *time* is immediately preceded by the word *no*). However, I *can* get you moving in a forward-focused direction by the end of this book—and isn't forward-focused the direction in which we *all* want to be heading?

One note of caution: the talk will get tough along the way, and there is an excellent rationale behind tough talking. Years ago, a fantastic mentor of mine once said, "I can be good to you or I can be good *for* you." I choose to be good *for* you, which occasionally entails taking off the velvet gloves and talking the tough talk (which is code for being honest). The good news is that my honesty is coming from a place of compassion, understanding, and most importantly, from someone who has walked a path similar to yours.

What I do *not* want to see is anyone becoming comfortable in a place of grief, sorrow, emptiness, or despair. I do *not* want anyone thinking, *I guess this widowhood thing is it for me,* and thereafter choosing to settle for . . . well, *settling.* Too many widowed who are grieving their loss or who are suffering through challenges along their healing journey will choose to settle simply because (a) they don't know how to take the first steps forward, (b) they were doing fine for a while and then something or someone hung them up to the point where they now feel "stuck," or (c) they are listening to the wrong people, those with negative opinions who are exerting way too much influence that generally yield counterproductive results. Frankly, you may have found yourself in a very sad sort of comfort zone—and if making that current comfort zone of sorrow just a little uncomfortable is what it takes to get you moving forward, I am more than happy to do so.

Following is your very first Boot Camp Affirmation to copy, stick to your bathroom mirror, paste to your forehead, or otherwise keep in front of you as much as possible.

> I'm still here. Although I face the daily challenge that is widowhood, it's because I am still here that makes me automatically entitled to the life that I truly want to live, in the ways that I wish to live it. I will not feel guilty in pursuing complete healing. I will not question my right to present and future happiness (however that happiness manifests), nor will I permit anyone else to question that right. Going forward, I will live with the determination that settling for less than the life that I choose to design for myself will never be an option.

The reason that you picked up this book is simple: you do not wish to postpone your healing journey any longer. As with most who are grieving, you may have had little or no control over the circumstances of your loss—but you have control *now*. Decide right *now* to truly feel the entitlement that this affirmation is giving to you. Breathe it deeply in. Let it into your heart. *Believe* it. *Own* your healing journey. *Own* this thing called life. Wake up every day with this intention and this sense of entitlement, and let *no one* take either away from you. *Now* is the time. *Today* is the day.

Boot Camp Challenge

Share your commitment to this very special Boot Camp with at least one other uplifting and positive person in your life, who will genuinely support you on your healing journey. Sharing creates accountability and it also invites the support that you will need along the way. Plus, whether you realize it or not, you may be sharing with a person who needs Bereavement Boot Camp just as badly as you do.

I am going to share my commitment to Bereavement Boot Camp with:

_____

The reason that I have chosen _____

is _____

_____

_____

_____

_____

How I feel after sharing: _____

_____

_____

_____

_____

EKITA!

Grief is not measured by clocks or calendars.
Grief is not measured by propinquity or geography.
Grief is not defined by blood, family trees, or lack thereof.
Grief is not a competition as to who is hurting worse.

❤

Grief is not a privilege,
only to be granted to those deemed "worthy" of grieving.
Grief is not hierarchical.
Grief cannot be quantified, nor need it be justified.

❤

Grief is measured by one thing and one thing only:
love.
Grief is measured by love:
love's heights and its depths.
Its give-and-take.
Its inexplicability . . . and its perfect sense.

❤

Grief is measured by love.
It's our way of reconciling the knowledge that
while life will never again be the same,
we'll strive to go on . . .

without knowing exactly how that will happen.
Or what life will look like
beyond the misty veil of tears.

♥

Grief is measured by love.
It's knowing why we must go on,
while figuring out how to go on . . .
one hour at a time.

♥

Grief is measured by love.
The love that we gave to another.
The love that was returned in kind.
The myriad memories created and celebrated,
and the forever imprint left on our hearts and in our souls
when we bade one another goodbye.
Grief is measured by love,
and love is the only measurement that matters.

CHAPTER

2

Embracing the "New" You

The widowed community generally spends a lot of time talking about how much their late spouses are missed. Not only is this completely and totally normal, it is also a welcome catharsis and a necessary factor in moving through the grieving process.

But in the midst of missing your spouse, do you ever miss *you?* Be honest. I know I miss me. Or rather, the person to whom I refer as "Pre-Widow Carole." Sometimes I *really* miss her. I miss the person I was before an evil illness named ALS invaded our home, unpacked its horrible baggage, settled in, and hijacked our lives. I miss the person I was before that evil stole a husband and father away from his family. The person I was before a thick darkness cloaked and enveloped us.

Permit me to introduce you to Pre-Widow Carole. She was a lot of fun. She was fun and flirty and laughed easily, loudly, and often. She ate pizza for breakfast, made people laugh, and wondered what she was going to wear to go out on Friday Night Date Night with her man. Just as with her parents' house before her own, Pre-Widow Carole boasted the hangout house at which the neighborhood kids loved to congregate. She was the fun mom: giver of slumber parties, holiday parties, birthday parties, makeover parties, cheerleader parties, back-to-school parties, and anything else involving the word *party*.

She trusted people readily, for no one had ever before given her any real reason to be otherwise.[1] Pre-Widow Carole had a lot more patience; with everything and everyone and with tiny little annoyances and great big crises. She was not afraid of life or love or much of anything. Pre-Widow Carole was, indeed, pretty cool.

Then Post-Widow Carole showed up—and I didn't like her very much at first.

She wasn't a lot of fun to be around. Not. At. All. The frivolity and the lightness had completely disappeared. Smiles, when they happened, were pasted-on masks that hid anguish and despair behind the façades. Laughter was rare.

It seemed like Post-Widow Carole complained a lot—about pretty much everything. She was an embittered woman, stung by both the grief of loss and the subsequent betrayal and abandonment of many of those previously mentioned people she once trusted implicitly. Post-Widow Carole did not seem to have much patience anymore, for anything. A lengthy stoplight, a long line at the grocery checkout . . . it did not take much to set her off on

---

1 Except for a few ex-boyfriends and a lot of first dates—but that's another story.

a profanity-filled rant. And Post-Widow Carole is *always* afraid. Anxious. On edge. Never one to worry needlessly and previously making fun of those who did, Post-Widow Carole seemed to now worry constantly about *all* things large and small: letting her (adult) daughters out of her sight; the cat sleeping too much; who might die next. All in all, Post-Widow Carole seemed like one great big drag on everything and everyone around her.

One day, I took another good look at Post-Widow Carole. I looked past all the not-so-great stuff and examined a few other things about Post-Widow Carole that differed from Pre-Widow Carole. Post-Widow Carole had cared for and buried a husband . . . and somehow managed to survive and rebuild from the emotional and financial devastation of it all. This Carole helped her daughter find her way through the depths of her own grief and back into the light of a childhood that had been postponed for years by the evil illness that once ruled the household. Post-Widow Carole is stronger than Pre-Widow Carole ever thought she could be. She offers a steely resolve that lets the world around her know that it might knock her down. But she will never *stay* down. This Carole will never cut-and-run when the going gets tough. The people closest to her can rely on that certainty without any doubt or question.

Post-Widow Carole does not trust quite as readily or implicitly as Pre-Widow Carole once did, because abandonment and betrayal are difficult and unwelcome experiences. However, difficult and unwelcome experiences can also be disguises for life lessons from which we can learn and benefit. More importantly, Post-Widow Carole still believes in the inherent good in people and, as a result, now counts many new, loving, and wonderful friendships that will last a lifetime. She learned to leave bitterness behind, because bitterness gnaws at the soul and drains energy that is better spent elsewhere in positive and productive ways. She embraced the fact that the reason she is so anxious and afraid of losing loved ones is because anxiety and fear are part of the cost of loving passionately and deeply. She realized how lucky she is to have that kind of love in her life: with her friends, her family, her children . . . and with a man who turned out to be a shining beacon in the darkness.

Post-Widow Carole learned what is worth fighting about and over, and when to simply walk away. And life got a lot easier.

I realize that because I am now a completely different person than I was pre-widowhood, some of that post-widow stuff is not going to change. My patience level is still pretty low. I do not trust as readily. I am still almost irrationally afraid of losing those whom I love so very much. I suppose that in some ways I will always miss Pre-Widow Carole, for I will never again be that person. But all in all, Post-Widow Carole is not so bad. In fact . . . she is kind of cool, too.

So, what about *you?* What do *you* miss about Pre-Widowed You? And what do *you* love about Post-Widowed You? It's okay to miss Pre-Widowed You and the life that you had before you lost your beloved. Why wouldn't you? However, you must also realize that you can't go through the widowhood experience and not be changed forever. You are not the same person anymore. You can't be. It's impossible.

Look in the mirror and take a look at who is staring back at you. I mean *really* look. I know that you either are experiencing or have experienced some of the worst pain that you will ever realize.

But I also strongly encourage you to truly embrace Post-Widowed You. Strength you did not realize you had. New relationships that you have welcomed. The life into which you are learning to move forward.

Embrace Post-Widowed You . . . because I know that Post-Widowed You is someone whom *I* would like to embrace—if for no other reason than to let you know that while Pre-Widowed You may be gone forever . . .

Post-Widowed You is pretty cool, too.

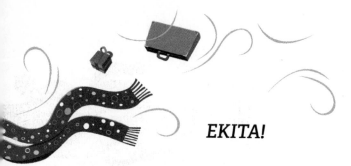

EKITA!

Grief is the tremendous price that we pay
when we love fully, passionately,
joyfully, and unconditionally;
with abandon and without measure or limits.
It's an admittedly painful and difficult cost,
but how empty life would be
if we chose against paying that price
and instead kept our love locked away
forever in our hearts?

CHAPTER

CHAPTER
3

Okay, God,...
Now What?

When I began my career as a writer in the grief-recovery genre, I made a very conscious decision to write from a place of secularity. My reasons for this decision were many. First, there are numerous and wonderful books on the market by experts in the area of spirituality as it pertains to grief recovery, and I prefer to leave subjects that require expert insight to those specific experts. Further, while I recognize that no one author can write for and appeal to absolutely every reader on the planet, I wanted to reach as many readers as possible—and the reality is that many people who have either experienced loss, are about to experience loss, or are currently going through loss are (a) not of a spiritual nature, or (b) seriously pissed off at a God whom they perceive as having betrayed them by putting them through unimaginable pain.

For the purposes of this discussion, let's define spirituality as it pertains to healing. Spirituality does not necessarily involve organized, "labeled" religion. It does not necessarily involve a house of worship or certain prayers at certain times of the hour, day, month, or year. Spirituality is whatever you seek and/or practice that brings you a sense of joy, enlightenment, comfort, solace, peace, knowledge expansion, or whatever it is that you seek as a boost and complement to your life in general, and your healing journey specifically. Keeping this in mind, I will be referring to houses of worship, my cleric, and my own personal spiritual study as anecdotal reference *only*. Please do not interpret these references as preaching or proselytizing, because I neither believe in, nor do I participate in, either practice.

This discussion is also not about the specifics of any particular religion; rather, it is about our own personal spirituality, our pursuit of spirituality, our questioning of faith and spirituality through what may be one of the darkest times in our lives, and how we might possibly integrate our spirituality—in any way, shape, or form—into our healing journeys. As you continue to read, you can mentally substitute what I am sharing with your own particular spiritual references.

A Spiritual Meltdown

My own journey in reconciling spirituality with grief was not always smooth or crystal clear. Indeed, I had always believed myself to be a spiritual person and had been so throughout my entire life. However, once my spirituality was tested as never before . . . well, things got a bit complicated.

Let me take you back to the day of Mike's diagnosis. As coincidence would have it, we were at the doctor's office receiving that wretched diagnosis in the morning, and I was to be in synagogue that evening for the beginning of Yom Kippur, the Day of Atonement. For those who may be unfamiliar, Yom Kippur is the holiest and most solemn day on the Jewish calendar. It's when we stand before God to be judged, to ask forgiveness for our sins and failings of the previous year, and to pledge to God and ourselves to strive to be better people in the upcoming year—to our families, to our friends and loved ones, to our colleagues, and to humankind. It is actually my favorite Jewish holiday because it calls for us to do the one thing that we rarely do in the course of our busy lives: we are made to *stop.*

Through cessation of work and through fasting, prayer, introspection, and retrospection, we are compelled to bring our electronically ruled, digitally dictated, overworked, and overscheduled lives to a twenty-four hour halt. It is a beautiful time of year that I truly treasure.

So it was just a few hours prior to the beginning of Yom Kippur that Mike and I were in a doctor's private study, the two of us seated on one side of a colossal mahogany desk and the doctor on the other. The doctor rose from his chair, came around the desk, sat down on the edge, leaned forward, and placed a compassionate hand on Mike's shoulder. He then ruefully looked into Mike's eyes and pronounced his diagnosis of an incurable and subsequently terminal illness. No one had to translate any medical lingo for me. I knew exactly what that diagnosis meant: Mike was going to die.

That was it. No surgeries, no treatments, no reassurances, no promises—no hope. Our future was finished, over before it had even arrived. There was nothing for us left to do, except pray that he would be around for a longer period of time . . . and, as cruel fate would have it, even *that* faint hope was ultimately dashed.

As one would naturally expect, the doctor said all of the typically encouraging things, i.e., "We're going to fight this; we're not giving up so don't you give up," and so forth. However, no matter what the doctor said or how cheerful a veneer he attempted, we all knew what that horrible diagnosis meant:

My Michael—my husband, loving daddy, and my best buddy of almost twenty years—was going to die . . . and it was going to be sooner rather than later.

After feeling like we had each been hit in our stomachs with wooden planks, we left the doctor's office, clinging to each other tightly, as if to hold one another up. Slowly and silently, we walked outside, heading to the car and not looking at one another; both lost in the hellish fog that was our initial shock, and trying desperately to absorb both the news that we had just received, and the prospect of what our lives were about to become.

Once home, and still not quite knowing what to say to one another, Mike gamely encouraged me to go to evening services, acting as though our world had not just imploded on us, and believing with all of his heart that going to services would be of comfort and help to me.

Boy, was he mistaken.

The Red Mist

In no mood to socialize either prior to or immediately after the service (never mind the intervening two hours), I nonetheless attended synagogue as Mike had quite forcefully suggested. Rather than genuinely absorbing the warmth, beauty, and peace of the lovely evening service and reverent commencement of this most holy period of time, on this night, I instead sat in the congregation, with my arms firmly crossed and with an expression on my face that I am positive could only be described as stone-like. Pissed off would not even begin to describe my inner churnings. I was incensed. I. Was. *Enraged.*

I was supposed to be in a prayerful place in my mind and heart, preparing to spiritually renew myself for the upcoming New Year, and the only thing that I felt was pure, through-and-through, unadulterated, organic anger. The worst part was that there was no one at whom to scream. There was no blame to be assessed for Mike's diagnosis; no fingers to point at guilty parties, no direction at which to hurl obscenities. I had nothing and no one on whom to take out my rage and my feelings of complete and absolute helplessness and hopelessness.

So I blamed God. I got well and truly mad at Him. Boiling mad. The British refer to it as "red mist," and that is precisely what I was—"red-mist" mad. I blamed God for absolutely everything connected with and to Mike's illness and the complete wreck that this illness had already made and was going to make out of all of our lives.

My life flashed through my mind like a movie on fast-forward. I began my religious education at the age of six years and, as I was taught to do, I spent my entire life working hard to be a good daughter, a good sister, a good student, and a good Jew. I became a Bat Mitzvah at thirteen years of age and ceremonially took my place as an adult in the Jewish community. As I grew through my teens and into young adulthood, I continued to be a good student, both practically and spiritually, and eventually became a good employee, a good wife, and a good mother. I had married a man who spent twenty-eight years on dangerous and unforgiving streets, serving and protecting the community. Prior to those twenty-eight years in service to the community, he had put on a military uniform and served his country in the United States Air Force, service that included two tours of duty in Vietnam.

So, instead of praying on that holiest of evenings, that stinking fast-forward movie was running as a continual loop through my mind. I was helpless to shut it off. Over and over, I kept asking both myself and God:

Why him? Why us? Why does he have to suffer? Why are we now going to be having conversations about life support and burial plans and last wishes? We're supposed to be planning our future and living our life—not dreading the future and planning his death. Okay God, you've handed this to us . . . what the hell are we supposed to do now?

I got into that mindset, dug thoroughly into that headspace, set up my own personal Angry and Bitter Camp, and remained there for the better part of two years, singing the "Why Me Blues" to anyone who would listen.

Why Not You?

Several months later and still firmly ensconced in Angry and Bitter Camp, I was again railing away and singing the "Why Us" verse of the "Why Me Blues" to our rabbi. He listened patiently and then quietly responded to my ranting with a reply that I didn't like much—and you won't like it either. He looked at me and in a very matter-of-fact tone asked, "Why *not* you?"

I looked at this man like he had two heads; trying with all my might not to go completely nuclear on him. How *dare* he say something so insensitive! Why *not*? I had just very sanctimoniously delivered an entire list of "why nots" (identical to the list that I have just shared with you). We are wonderful people. We are wonderful partners, and we are wonderful parents. My husband is a fantastic human being. What do we receive in return for all of our collective wonderfulness? Our life as a family is being destroyed. Our nine-year-old daughter gets to watch her daddy die by inches. I am pretty damn sure that we do not deserve to have this happen . . . to *us*.

After calmly listening to my indignation, the rabbi then posed a very interesting question: "If not you, who should this be happening to instead? Think of all of the good, decent, loving people you know who are just like you and tell me, if not you, who *does* deserve this? Pick a family you know and tell me that they deserve this."

As much as I hated to admit it, he was absolutely right. Who indeed deserves such a fate? On whom would *any* of us wish our respective tragedies?

Now, I would love to tell you that at that very moment, I saw the brilliantly bright light of reason, that the skies parted and the angels sang their angel chorus[1] and the anger magically melted away, and I was smiling and benevolent and filled with understanding from that point forward.

Not exactly.

I truly wish I were that evolved, but as I always teach, you cannot tell someone how to feel. Although the rabbi's words made

---

1 In my head, this is usually Beethoven's Symphony No. 9, "Ode to Joy."

perfect sense to my intellect, I know that you will agree when I say that the distance between the brain and the heart is approximately ten million miles. The rabbi may have made all the sense in the world to my brain; however, my heart was still broken—and I was still really, *really* angry. So I remained in the tent that I had pitched in Angry and Bitter Camp and remained livid at everything in general and nothing in particular.

The Epiphany (Happily) Strikes

Fast-forward two years . . . While on my last business trip prior to Mike's death, I decided to take advantage of some down time in my hotel room with one of my brand-new "how-to Jew" books[2] that I had brought with me. Among other interpretations of various liturgies, this particular book contained a short summary of the Book of Job. As you may know (and I'm paraphrasing, so hang in there), Job is a really great guy, doing all the right things, and he has it all—great family, great wealth, and great success. Everything is going just great . . . until everything is taken away from him, testing his faith in God. His buddies and even his wife are telling him to turn away from God (who they think is messing with him), yet Job continues to keep his faith. When Job finally does get a little curious and says to God, "What's up with all this tragedy that I'm being made to endure?" God responds by asking Job, "Did you create the earth? Did you separate day from night and manage to get all this other cool stuff done?" What God is essentially saying

---

2 An affectionate term I coined for books that explain a variety of Judaic aspects, from traditions and customs to biblical interpretation and explanations as to the "whys" and "hows" of Judaism, even modern twists on holiday observations and old-school recipes. To continually expand knowledge in our spirituality is to continually grow and learn, hence, my term "how-to Jew."

is, "I know what I'm doing, and if you hang in there with me, things are going to be okay." As the story goes, Job did continue his walk in faith and was eventually rewarded with even more abundance than what was originally lost.

Though it is obviously paraphrased, this particular synopsis spoke to me in a way that I had never before experienced—and isn't that the very definition of faith? For me, faith is that which speaks to you and touches you and moves you and provokes you to think and question and seek and discover that which, in the end, reinforces *your* particular faith.

I felt like I'd discovered painless high heels or the secret to eating French bread without gaining weight. I honestly felt like a light came on in my life. Excitedly, I called my rabbi back in California and told him that I got it. I *finally* got it.

While I realized that our particular end result was not going to change, and I did not like the end result that we were facing any better, at least I *got* it. I had finally figured out that God was not some vicious mischief-maker, looking down from on high and thinking, *Hmm, who can I mess with? I know . . . I'll mess with the Fleet family.*

After again patiently listening to my animated babbling and upon asking him why on earth he had kept this amazing "secret" from me, the rabbi said (and this is very important), "I'm so glad that you got it—but this is something that you had to come to by yourself. I couldn't have told you this or any other story and expected to change your mind about your feelings. You had to make this discovery for yourself. You had to get to this place on your own."

I realized how right he was. Spiritual understanding and reconciliation of spirituality with loss and grief is a place that you have to get to on *your* own and on *your* terms. However, in order to get there, *you* have to do the exploration. To find the answers, you first have to actually *look* for answers.

After my telephone conversation with the rabbi, I spoke with one of my colleagues later that evening.[3] In sharing this epiphany with her, it occurred to me that I had spent the better part of two years being really angry at God, and in that anger I had said some pretty awful things to Him. Because of the depth of my anger, I couldn't even be bothered to be in a prayerful place with God on the holiest day of the year. I felt so very guilty. Would God even bother listening to me after the rage that I had unleashed on and entirely directed to and at Him?

My colleague listened closely to my concerns and then said something so brilliant that I have quoted it ever since. She said, "Don't worry, Carole—whatever anger you have been unloading all over God, He's big enough to handle it." I believe she is absolutely right.

Obviously, this stunning revelation of mine did not alter our reality. Two months after my epiphany, Mike still died. I was still left a widowed parent facing enormous financial and emotional challenges, and Kendall and I still faced a long and difficult road of recovery and healing. The difference was that I was not angry at God anymore, and, in resolving my spiritual anger, I was able to resolve my secular anger as well. By exploring my spirituality and working toward reconciling the anger, I was better equipped to mourn the loss, go through the grieving process, help my daughter with her processes, and help both of us heal with an open mind and open heart to what my faith had been teaching me all along.

---

3 Seriously. I was *really* excited about this,

It is important to emphasize that experiencing this spiritual epiphany doesn't mean that I no longer get angry at life or at God. Since Mike's death, there are plenty of times when I sit down and have a bit of a chat with God, usually beginning with the words, "Okay, I *really* need an explanation for this." In the course of said chat, I know full well that I am not going to get an explanation and, even if I did, it would not immediately change the situation. However, God has never once asked me or anyone else not to be human or not to have human feelings, frailties, and failings—anger among them. In my heart, I know that what He asks of me is that I continue walking in faith and exploring and questioning and studying, because when I do, things generally improve and answers are eventually revealed. They are not always the answers that I want, but you know what? When I was young, I didn't always get the answers that I wanted from my parents either. My feeling is that God really *does* answer all prayers—it's just that, like it or not, sometimes the answer is not yes.

During times of loss, many of us question our faith, whatever that faith may be. Many of us have more than a few moments of anger, along with a whole bunch of unanswered questions, the first of which is usually, "Why me?"—and that is okay. To me, the greater pity would have been if I had stayed in Angry and Bitter Camp or in endless mourning or in whatever place that might have prevented me from moving forward into a life of renewed happiness.

The Lesson...and the Answer to "Now What?"

So, after the big epiphany and after Mike's death, instead of spending any more time on "Why *me?*" (a question that will not be answered while I'm walking the earth, and one that doesn't keep me on a positive path), I started focusing on "What *now*?" I began my days by asking myself, *"What am I going to do today to help myself and Kendall heal and continue forward?"* The lesson here is that while asking, "Why *me*" is a perfectly normal and natural reaction to tragedy, *staying* in a "Why *me*" mindset does absolutely nothing to change the situation. Deciding instead to work on the "What now" ... *will!* In other words, I decided to reach up as far as I could—and I believe that when I do that, God will reach down the rest of the way. I definitely took the scenic route to get to that belief space (the long way around, if you will), but I was eventually able to integrate my spirituality into my grief recovery.

Even if you are angry at God right now and are questioning Him and/or everything about your faith—and remember, I am someone who spent a full two years that way—turning inward and into your faith to get both perspective and direction can really work. Have you integrated your spirituality into your grief recovery? Or have you experienced a crisis of faith similar to what I described?

Experiencing a crisis of faith is 100 percent normal and perfectly okay. Obviously, so is *not* experiencing a crisis of faith, and, if that is you, you have my admiration. If you have indeed experienced a crisis of faith (either now or in the past), *please* do not feel guilty, as you have nothing to feel guilty about. Understand that a *crisis* of faith is not an *abandonment* of faith; there is a huge difference. A crisis of faith is merely your way of questioning what has happened to you versus your faith and how to reconcile an earthly event with your own spiritual relevance. I encourage you to turn into your faith, even if you are in a place of anger or doubt. Talk to those within your faith; both your fellow spiritual community members and experts; be they priests or pastors, rabbis or reiki masters, bishops or elders or imams or gurus—whoever is in a position to knowledgeably, wisely, compassionately, and sensitively help guide you to a place of peace.

Sending the Thank-You Note, Praying "Just Because," and the Matter of Perfect Timing

Let me ask you a question: when do you pray?

I mean *really* pray?

Do you pray only during times of trial? Do you pray only when you are in a house of worship? Do you pray only when you really need your NFL team to pull through in a must-win game?

When God answers your prayers to your advantage, happiness, and benefit, do you ever send the "thank-you note"? I did not always remember the thank-you note . . . but I do now.

We all pray in times of trial or want.

We pray that our ill family members and loved ones will be healed.

We pray that traffic will be light, or that the rain will hold off until after the outdoor event, or that the dress we love comes in our perfect size.

We pray that we receive the job offer or the raise.

We pray that our children remain safe.

But do you ever pray "just because?"

I did not always pray "just because" . . . but I do now.

Do you love hearing about "God's timing?" Because I don't. God's timing and my timing rarely seem to coincide.

I want what I want when I want it. I need what I need when I need it.[4] Yet, most of the time, God seems to have other ideas . . . until He reveals the reason(s) why His timing is the way that it is . . . at which time I inevitably say, "Oh, now I get it."

I never truly understood God's timing—but I do now.

Following are a few quick suggestions on how to enrich your own spirituality as it pertains to your healing journey:

1. **By all means, pray during the tough times, but don't forget to send the thank-you note.** When you pray during times of trial or difficulty, remember to say "thank you" after your troubled waters have calmed. Look at it this way: when we were young, we were always taught to write a thank-you note after receiving a gift. Our answered prayers are a gift, wouldn't you agree?

   Remember to say thank you when you receive those gifts. If the answer to your prayer appears to be "No" or "Not right now," send the thank-you note anyway. It will help you to feel a sense of center and serve as a reminder to be grateful for what exists in your life.

2. **Pray "just because."** Do you get annoyed when the only time you hear from certain people is when they want or need something from you? Me too. So why do so many of us pray only when we need or want something from God? Why do we pray only when we are in our houses of worship? How about praying just because? For me, that means sitting down at the end of the day (quietly and with no distractions) and spending just a few minutes with scriptural interpretations,

---

4 Understanding that the word "need" is an entirely subjective term.

affirmations, inspirational passages, or meditation. No requests are made, no lists of needs, wants, or have-to-haves. It is prayer and devotion "just because." Give it a try and see if you notice a peace coming over you.

3. **Get some patience with God's timing.** This is the toughest part of all, at least it is for me. While I have many virtues, patience is admittedly not among them. However, when I release my own insistence on timing and try to tune in a little more to God's timing (or to "Let go and let God"), I feel much less aggravated, a lot more peaceful, and far more open to seeing what God's timing eventually reveals.

4. **Don't forget to consult the experts.** Talk to your cleric or spiritual leader about how you're feeling right now and about your faith as it pertains to your healing journey. Even if you were or are as angry as I was (and I am sure that there is at least one of you out there), your spiritual leader is in a position to guide you knowledgeably, wisely, and with compassion and understanding. Combined with your Bereavement Boot Camp assignments, your cleric or spiritual leader may also give you a few assignments or direction to augment your journey. Imagine the potentially powerful combination *that* could be!

EKITA!

You can honor your past,

you can treasure your past,

you can and you certainly should love your past . . .

you don't have to *live* in the past.

♥

Life is not an either/or proposition.

You don't have to choose between

yesterday and tomorrow.

♥

Bring your past forward with you . . .

into the new life that you are building

and will again learn to love.

CHAPTER

4

Bereavement
Boot Camp Lesson Two:
"My Healing Journey
Is *Mine*"

Welcome to your second Boot Camp lesson. This chapter's theme serves as an important reminder and one that every single one of us needs to hear periodically. Let's begin with the bottom line: your healing journey belongs to no one else but *you*. Given that your healing journey belongs to only you, any insight or opinions that *are not* supportive, helpful, encouraging, or will help to take you in the forward-focused direction in which you wish to go are automatically irrelevant.

Unfortunately, many people (both the widowed and those who surround them) too often compare their own journeys to both the methods and speeds of other people's perceived recoveries, or to other loss experiences in general. Worse, there may be people around you who are so uncomfortable with your grief that they really just want you to "hurry up already." This generally manifests itself in the incredibly overused (and insensitive) phrase:

"You should be over it by now."[1]

It's perfectly okay to roll your eyes.

The problem here is twofold. First, there is absolutely no such thing as getting "over it."[2] Second, the people who are in need of support are oftentimes listening to people saying things like "Get over it"—and taking them seriously.

Hear me clearly, please: in addition to being just plain wrong, listening to people who have no idea what you are going through or what they are talking about is not going to be helpful to or for you.

The sad reality is that a large majority of people coping with loss have heard "Get over it" at least once during a healing journey. Now, what happens when you hear these words? Inside, you may be thinking, *"Well, I'm not over it, so clearly there is something wrong with me."* Here's what happens: Your brain functionality locks right into the *"There's something wrong with me"* part of the negative thought process, and that is exactly where your focus goes. You begin to think that something *is* wrong with you.

The fact is that the people who are telling you to "get over it" (and ultimately deny you ownership of and control over your healing journey) are not at all interested in what is best for you. Rather, it would be easier for *them* if you get over it. It would be easier for *them* if you "hurry up" with the grieving portion of your loss

---

1 (. . . or words to that effect).

2 The phrase is a complete myth, along with "time healing all wounds" and a few other myths that need to be immediately abolished, many of which we will be discussing later.

program because *they* do not want to deal with you or your grief. It is easier for *them* if you would just please conform to *their* healing timeline, which, by the way, is the timeline that they are using to dictate to you. Most of all, they are straight up uncomfortable with *you*.

What do the Get-Over-Its want? They want you to be the person you were *before*—before loss invaded your life; before what once was two became one, and before you quit being "fun" and had to take a desperately needed and vitally important time-out to figure out who you are now and what the hell you are supposed to do with this life that you have been handed.

Many do not realize that it is completely impossible for you to be the person that you were "before" because, as you know, a loss of this caliber forever changes you. Furthermore, and though we certainly would not wish misfortune on anyone, until or unless the negative people around you experience a life-altering set of circumstances, they are not likely to be stricken with a sudden case of compassion for that which you are going through and your sincere efforts to move through that particular set of circumstances to a place of peace. The facts are these—please pay attention:

- ✓ Not everyone is going to "get" you.
- ✓ Not everyone is going to understand you.
- ✓ Not everyone is going to be appropriately sympathetic to your plight.
- ✓ Not everyone is going to approve of who you are, what you say, what you do, or how you go about doing it; especially when it comes to your healing journey. You will learn much more about this concept in Boot Camp Lesson Five.

There is no denying that words cut as sharply as any knife. However, you must remember that a negative opinion is both momentary and unimportant. Come to think of it, negative people in general are unimportant; as such, they *cannot* become any kind of an influencing factor on your healing journey. I further promise you this: *No one* is sitting around at home or at work thinking about how you are handling your healing journey or anything connected with it. People are far more concerned with their own lives, yet you might be letting negative opinions affect or outright interfere with *your* journey. You must realize that this is how negative people operate—they venture unsolicited and useless opinions and then quickly move on to find someone else on whom to foist their unwelcome insight.

Understanding the likelihood that most of the people in your life really *do* care about you and have your best interests at heart, there will always be people around you who will want you to be over it quickly because of their discomfort with your grief. If—or when—you do get fed up with the same person (or people) telling you what to do, what not to do, or how you should conduct any part of your healing journey, simply smile and ask, "How's your widowhood going for you?" This is a line that I finally mustered up the courage to utter just over one year into my own journey. You don't have to be rude, but you can be very clear in letting them know exactly who is in charge of your healing journey and that they should perhaps back off a bit.

What *is* the fastest way to total grief recovery? Not trying to be "fast" about it. After you embrace that you never "get over it" (you instead move *forward* from the experience), commit to taking the time and the steps that you need to take to recover in *your* own way and in *your* own time. Stay true to *you*. Commit to surrounding yourself with the positivity and support that is out there in any and all forms. Negative people need not apply to be a part of your life, nor should they be granted a place of prominence in it. You have healing to do and you *can* do this.

Here is your second Boot Camp Affirmation. Keep it in front of you.

My healing journey belongs to no one else. I cannot and will not be compared to other people, and my loss cannot and will not be compared to any other loss experiences, including my own. Even though there may be people around me who wish I would do otherwise, I cannot and will not hurry my grief or my grieving processes, nor will I make any attempts to do so. I accept that healing after this level of loss is neither fast, nor is it easy; therefore, I will truthfully honor whatever it is that I am feeling when I am feeling it rather than let others dictate how I should or should not be feeling.

Boot Camp Challenge

It is now time to honor how you are feeling at this point on your journey. Everyone seeks their comfort in different ways, and you are going to choose to do something that brings a smile to your face and warmth to your heart.

Within the next week, set aside time (at least twice) to do something that will bring you a measure of comfort. The specific activity and the time investment are entirely up to you. It can be as little as twenty minutes to yourself, or it can be a full day or two. You can spend this special time with a close friend or choose to spend it alone. This time might include anything from spending time with your faith to visiting a favorite coffee house, bookstore, or scenic area near your home. It could be working out to really loud music (which is how I choose to cope) or taking the time to prepare a lovely meal just for yourself. The important thing to remember is that this is about honoring your authentic feelings and shutting out any opinions that do not support your efforts to move forward.

Within the next week, I am going to _____ at least _____ times within the next week. I am planning to spend _____ per day, understanding that more days and/or more time can be added.

How I feel now: _____

_____

_____

_____

_____

_____

_____

How I feel afterward: _____

_____

_____

_____

_____

_____

_____

_____

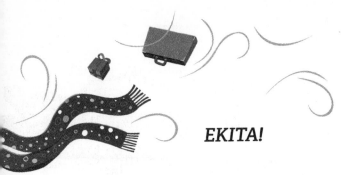

EKITA!

Coal becomes diamonds because of pressure.

Oysters produce pearls because of irritation.

It's then no wonder that

we refer to the widowed as precious gems.

Why?

Because the widowed have been through all of that

... and then some.

CHAPTER

5

Grief... or Relief?

Since I began working in and with the bereaved community many years ago, I have always made it a personal goal to reach as many people in need as possible. I feel that ours should be a wholly inclusive community, understanding and embracing each person's individual circumstances surrounding their widowhood. Let me also remind you that I do not intentionally court controversy, nor have I ever gone out of my way to be intentionally controversial. I can't even stomach confrontation (real or fictional) on television. I will therefore never be the one who is controversial for the sake of getting attention or for shock value, the latter of which seems to be more and more on-trend these days. In my mind, seeking controversy or spouting off "shocking" statements for the sake of attention is tantamount to throwing a "Look at me" temper tantrum—and I'm simply not inclined.

That said, there indeed do exist many aspects of widowhood that are considered controversial and are subsequently and too often ignored—situations that can lead to even greater feelings of marginalization and isolation. Because of this avoidance and marginalization, I have actually had widowed ask me if they are welcome to participate on my social media pages because they or their particular widowhood situations "aren't like everyone else."[1] For this and many other reasons, I refuse to dodge or altogether avoid these areas of so-called controversy, mostly because too many others choose to do just that. As I have long taught, *not* discussing uncomfortable issues does not make those issues disappear. It just keeps us in a place of ill-preparedness and leaves those who are dealing with the difficult, the awkward, the painful, or the scary left off to one side yet again—and I will not have it.

One of the seldom-discussed subjects surrounding widowhood concerns those widowed who are actually relieved when their spouses pass away. I realize that may sound like a heartless statement on its face, but let's delve just a little deeper into the subject. Much of what's written about grief recovery speaks to the great majority of widowed who are heartbroken after losing their spouses, and rightly so. However, what of the widowed who feel little to no grief at all? Quite the contrary, these widowed are relieved—even actually happy—that their spouses have passed away. However, because of both societal and religious mores and expectations, there is great difficulty in reconciling those feelings (let alone expressing those feelings outwardly). What is worse is that often accompanying these feelings are our old, familiar nemeses, *guilt* and *shame*. Think about it: what kind of human being

---

1 Of course, the answer is and will always be a resounding "YES!"

actually feels a sense of relief or even happiness upon losing their spouse?[2] The answer?

- ✓ Those who were the victims of ongoing domestic violence (because domestic violence rarely happens only once).
- ✓ Those who endured emotional and/or verbal abuse (which also does not happen only once).
- ✓ Those who lived with a substance abuser (alcohol, recreational drugs, or prescription drugs).
- ✓ Those who lived with someone who was financially irresponsible, led a financial double life, became a financial burden, or who was otherwise endangering or obliterating the financial security of the household.[3]
- ✓ Those who lived with infidelity (please see the "just once" explanations above).

So what do you do if the relieved widowed happens to be you? Where and to whom do you turn for support without fear of judgment or admonishment? Who can you trust to listen to your feelings without being met with "that look"? Who will truly understand your lack of devastation? How do you freely express yourself in and amongst a widowed community, whose members, by and large, are in mourning and waxing poetically and nostalgically about their beloved? Meet Martha, who had been planning to ask her husband for a separation after twenty years of marriage—then life hurled a huge curveball in her direction.

---

2 Obviously, there can be other issues that may take place within a marriage and/or a household that could easily be included on this list; however, these are the most common reasons behind feeling post-loss relief.

3 This does not mean someone who was unemployed through no fault of their own, or physically unable to work. I'm referring to someone who, for whatever reason, intentionally decided that they should not "have to" work, thereby leaving all financial responsibility and burden to their spouse.

Grief and Relief in the Same Space

Martha's Story:

There was no longer any love in our marriage, but instead a polite tolerance. There had been two instances of infidelity on his part and I couldn't get past that. The day we got word that he might have cancer, I was going to get on a plane for a work trip. While I was gone, I was going to figure out how to ask for a separation.

When my husband passed away, I did experience grief, but I also experienced relief. The grief was on behalf of our children, who were going to grow up without a father. I was relieved, because I no longer had to think about ending our marriage. Regardless of my sense of relief, there was still the loss of a long-term marriage, and the loss that my kids would be feeling for the rest of their lives. They were not privy to the issues between their dad and me, and I didn't want to change their image of their dad.

"Fronting" While Feeling Guilty

I felt very guilty feeling relief [that my husband had died]. I attended grief workshops, bereavement counseling and met with other widows. Everyone was in such a different place. Some couldn't seem to come to grips with their loss, while I was secretly thrilled that I was a widow. I have never shared these feelings except with my counselor. Over time, he has been able to help me see that I was not the problem in our marriage. My husband's issues had caused me to have low self-esteem, low self-worth, and to completely devalue myself. It has taken years for me to understand that we both had a part in our marriage taking the direction that it did.

Since the day he was diagnosed with cancer, I put on the façade of the loving wife who would stand by his side and fight along with him. I kept up that front after he died because I didn't want his memory ruined for the kids or any of our friends. But inside, the fact that I can't be honest about who he was and what our marriage was actually like has eaten me up.

Facing and Owning the Relief

For the first time, I am actually allowing myself to freely feel relieved. I still do not let the kids know that I am relieved their dad died, but I live my life more fully and wholly now. I am a completely changed person. People have noticed the changes but attribute it to "getting over" my loss.

There is generally a solid reason (or reasons) that a widowed person would feel relieved or even happy that their spouse has passed away. We must be understanding of those reasons and encourage these widowed—*all* of them—to step out of the shadows of self-imposed shame and into the light of healing and support. As we don't accept those who judge our individual journeys, so too must we be understanding and supportive of another widowed person's path, even if that journey involves feelings of respite and liberation rather than overwhelming sorrow.

Martha wisely advises, "Don't feel guilty for how you feel. Allow yourself to feel those feelings. Make sure you talk to a professional and work through those feelings though." She's absolutely correct in that a counselor, therapist, or grief expert can help you work through that which you may believe to be entirely "inappropriate" and, at the same time, perfectly justifiable feelings. Do not hesitate to seek professional help in dealing with your more specialized grief, and do not permit anyone to tell you how to feel, because how you feel *is how you feel.*

Most importantly, please don't be afraid of or avoid your community of support. We are here—and we truly care.

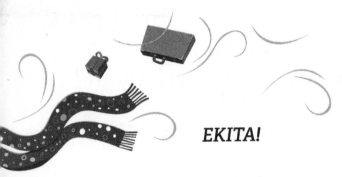

EKITA!

It's okay to stand apart
even if standing apart
means periodically
standing alone.

"How Long Were You Married?": Is *Any* Length of Time Enough?

July 22, 5:45 AM: I was awakened from a troubled sleep by the telephone call that our family had been expecting with a tremendous amount of dread. Expecting, yes, but dreading all the same: after a brave battle with a number of health issues, my beloved Uncle Harry had passed away.

Crying softly, I quietly slipped downstairs while the rest of the house remained asleep. I made myself a cup of my favorite English Breakfast tea and sat outside to watch dawn break across the canyon and over the mountains, while I contemplated how I was going to share this horrible news with Kendall and the rest of my family. As we all naturally do during times of loss, I then let my mind wander back to the lovely, halcyon days of my childhood.

Uncle Harry was a bit of a scallywag; a mischievous scamp, really. A "second daddy" to me, he was bold and bawdy and out-loud hilarious. As my cousin so beautifully put it, "Dad loved a good joke. He loved a bad one even more." And it was true. Uncle Harry loved a good practical joke—particularly if he was the one who played it, and especially when it was at the expense of the females in the family. And you can be sure that from the time I was permitted to date at the tender age of fifteen years to the very end of his life, *no* man I ever brought around the family was truly made to feel welcome without a stern looking up and down.[1]

Most of all, Uncle Harry had a gift that not too many people boast today. Uncle Harry listened. *Really* listened. Whenever he asked, "How are you?" it wasn't simply a pleasantry. He actually *wanted* to know how you were doing. He engaged. He took interest. He asked pertinent questions. He was always interested in what I was up to, where life was taking me next, and my opinions on everything. When I was sixteen years old, he wouldn't let me drive home from their house at night if he felt that the weather made driving too dangerous. When I was fifty years old, I endured intense questioning as to how I met my then-brand-new husband . . . and just as he did when I was younger, he concluded his line of "man-terrogation" with, "If he ever gives you any trouble, you just let me know."

And the thing is, he meant it. He *always* meant it.

He made me feel like I mattered, especially during a period of my adolescence when I was convinced that I did not matter. He made me feel worthwhile and important, even when I fell flat on my backside (and I have certainly done *that* more than once).

---

1 I'm not kidding. He would actually physically look these poor guys up and down, oftentimes with a look on his face like he smelled something bad.

For our family, Uncle Harry's death was the latest in a long line of overwhelming losses.

Since widowed generally get bombarded with calls and visits after the death of a spouse, I gave my Aunt Charlotte a few days to catch her breath before I called to check on her. She was doing about the same as anyone else is doing mere days after losing their beloved spouse. As we were talking and crying and even laughing together, Aunt Charlotte said something that struck me profoundly. She said that she kept asking herself, "*Why did this happen?*" Knowing all too well that this is a question that most widowed ask themselves, but that this question can also mean numerous different things, I asked Aunt Charlotte to explain what she meant. She replied, "I wasn't ready to lose him. I thought we would have another twenty years together. It wasn't time yet."

They were married for *fifty-three years.*

After my conversation with Aunt Charlotte, I thought about the countless letters I've received that say essentially the same thing.

- ✓ "We didn't have enough time together. It's not fair."
- ✓ "People say that I don't 'count' as a widow because we weren't together 'long enough.'"
- ✓ "I wasn't supposed to lose my husband/wife/partner after only _____" (fill in the blank).

While many of these letters are written by those who have been married a short period of time, I also receive many more letters written by widowed who were together twenty, thirty, and more than fifty years. People who were married for a short period of time will often hear ridiculous things like, "Perhaps you were meant to be alone," or, "You weren't married long enough to be this sad."; while people like my Aunt Charlotte who were married for longer periods of time will hear very "helpful" things like, "He lived a full life," and, *"Well, you had a long life together."*

Comforting? Not especially.

My dear Aunt Charlotte was the person who actually made me stop and ask myself, *How much time with your beloved is truly enough?*

The Short and the Long of It

One of the most common questions that the widowed are asked by those around them is, "How long were you married?" or, "How long were you together?" Many widowed who were with their beloveds for what's considered a shorter period of time then feel as though they have to justify themselves and their relationships, as if you are not actually widowed if you were not married "long enough," or if you were not technically married at all. What is really terrible is that there are people who are narrow-minded and insensitive enough to look at a grief-stricken widowed in the eye and opine as to whether or not their widowhood is "legitimate," based on nothing more than a piece of paper and/or a timetable.

Guess what? I do not care about what is or is not on paper. I don't care about legalities or technicalities, and I certainly don't care about length of time.[2] I also don't care about what anyone has to say based on these supposed "widowed barometers." Whether you were married or together as a couple for thirty years, thirty

---

[2] Stop right now, go back and re-read the very first EKITA in the book that begins with the sentence, "Grief is not measured by clocks or calendars." Enough said.

days, or thirty minutes, if you lost your beloved, the person to whom you were committed to spending the rest of your life, *you are widowed*. It's that simple. You don't have to justify yourself or your relationship to *anyone*.

The flip side of having to justify widowhood based upon an opinion of not being married long enough or not being legally married at all, are the widowed who were married for decades. A great majority of these widowed are greeted post loss with being told how "lucky" they are. Unfortunately, this can often leave a widowed person feeling as though they have no right to mourn their loss. After all, they were together for such a long time, so instead of feeling sad, they should be feeling only gratitude. While those like my Aunt Charlotte who were married or together for many years do generally feel grateful for having had those years, not one of them feels "lucky" during a time of loss.

Loss is not lucky—for *anyone*. I have yet to hear a widow/er say, "Yes, he/she's gone, but we were together for X amount of months/ years, and that was enough. I was completely ready for them to depart this earth and leave me all alone. Boy, am I lucky." Nope. I have not heard that statement even once.

We indeed feel grateful for the time that we had with our spouses, regardless of the length of that time. However, be it long or short, the length of time spent with our spouses is not a fair measurement for the level of love experienced or the level of grief felt upon losing them—and those left behind have the unequivocal right to mourn the loss.[3] It really is that simple.

So, as they have been doing for much of my life, Uncle Harry and Aunt Charlotte are still teaching me. Their life lesson compels

---

3 You will learn more in Chapter Fourteen, "The Inalienable Right to Grieve."

me to remind you that there is *no* amount of time that is or ever will be enough.

Regardless of the duration of your relationship, the loss of your beloved is *the loss of your beloved*. It is devastating on levels that you did not realize existed. If you were married for a shorter period of time, your time together still "counts" (in other words, you *are* a widow/er), and you obviously did not have the chronological time together that you richly deserved. If you were married for a longer period of time, you *still* did not have enough time together! Let no one imply that you are not entitled to mourn because you were together for many years and are therefore "lucky," or conversely, that you don't count as widowed because you did not have the opportunity to be married for decades.

No matter the amount of time you spent as a couple, you will always feel robbed and cheated out of even more time with your beloved because you were forced to say goodbye. No one is ever ready for that terrible day—or for that terrible goodbye.

Not even after fifty-three years.

While I always invite and encourage you to peacefully reflect on your time spent with your beloved, whatever that amount of time turned out to be, I will never tell you that your time together was enough. Don't let *anyone* tell you that your time together was enough. Because it wasn't enough.

And it never will be.

EKITA!

When it comes to your healing journey,
who are you *really* listening to?
Who are you permitting to inform and influence
one of the most important journeys of your entire life?

♥

Are you listening to those who lift you up and support you?
Are you listening to people in a position to help you,
be it practically, emotionally, mentally, or spiritually?
Are you even bothering to listen to *you*?

♥

Or are you listening to people who are negative,
condescending, or hurtful;
who have nothing helpful to say, offer, or contribute?
Sadly, too many are listening to the latter.
Before anyone else, you must first listen to *you*.
What is your inner voice telling you?
After you've listened to and truly heard your own voice,
you should thereafter listen to and pay heed only to the people who
are and will continue to contribute to your healing
and your life in constructive ways.
You have neither the time nor the energy for anything less.

When Grieving Becomes Dangerous: Stopping the Cycle of Destructive Coping

What is the first thing that goes through your mind when I reference "destructive coping?" You may very well think of what commonly goes through the minds of most—the abuse of alcohol and/or drugs in direct reaction to loss and subsequent grief and bereavement. While you would be sadly correct in that assumption, there are actually numerous other ways in which people choose to destructively cope with loss that have the capability to destroy both the lives of sufferers and those who love them. We now shine a great big white-hot spotlight on the most common destructive avenues that too many are either tempted to choose or are outright choosing as coping mechanisms to deal with loss.

One of the primary reasons that many go down a destructive coping path is that with the obvious exception of suicide, these practices have one common denominator: each momentarily feels good. Food, drink, shopping, sex—in moderation, are all enjoyable. The issues arise when the lines of moderation are crossed—and once moderation is breached, these same practices cease being merely pleasurable and instead become numbing agents against or escapism from grief. The crossed line subsequently casts sufferers headlong into destructive practices.

While each behavior carries individual consequences, the primary issue is that no matter how an escape or an "anesthetic" effect is achieved, once the feeling diminishes, the grief is still there. The pain is still there. The void left behind by the person who has died is still there. Worst of all, in addition to the grief and the pain and facing the void, you are also dealing with the consequences of destructive behavior, whether those consequences manifest as a sick-making hangover, a credit card bill that you have no way of paying—or something even more serious. The facts are these: no grief or pain will ever be resolved by coping destructively. No void can ever be filled by coping destructively. *Nothing* positive will ever come of coping destructively.

Another common ground between most destructive coping avenues is guilt, shame, and poor self-image, easily compounded by continued destructive coping. Shame is generally coupled with embarrassment, which is why many who cope destructively cannot bring themselves to ask for help. Poor self-image is not always born of loss, but if one is struggling with self-image (and many know that struggle), destructive coping will only feed that poor self-image.

Making distinctions between moderation and destructive coping can be challenging under normal circumstances. Now, add in the entire grieving process and the ability to make the distinction between moderation and problematic behavior can be extremely difficult. Deconstructing these behaviors is an important step in determining if you have a problem or if you are on your way to a problem.

Be it on paper, in the media, or in person, I have strictly warned against destructive coping too many times to count. We are now going to delve into what the umbrella of destructive coping can encompass, and what to do if you or someone you know is either currently coping destructively or is exhibiting tendencies toward coping in this manner.

Understand that when it comes to destructive coping, I will not quietly and gently steer you in the right direction. I will verbally push and prod and cajole you just as hard as I can in the right direction.[1] As is my habit, I begin by reminding you of a very important bottom line: Even if you are right now in the grips of destructive coping, even if you are engaging in more than one potentially destructive behavior, please know that . . .

You are *not* powerless.

You are *not* without control.

Destructive behavior does *not* own you.

If you are in immediate crisis, please don't hesitate to call 911 without delay. Additionally, you'll find a full complement of resources pertaining to each area of challenge (including contact information) in the back of the book.

---

1 Remember those references to "Boot Camp" and "Kicking Grief in the Ass?" I was not kidding.

When One Drink Is Too Many— and Ten Is Not Enough

Drinks after work at your local happy hour. A champagne toast at a wedding. A religious ritual. A cocktail before dinner. Alcohol is widely accepted as a natural and normal part of societal function. Factor in that alcohol is legal, readily available, and doesn't have to be expensive, it can become one of the easiest ways in which people choose to cope with loss.

I have borne personal witness to and have been directly impacted by the devastating effects of the alcoholism of loved ones and am all too familiar with the havoc that can be wrought, both on the abuser and those around them. The good news is that there is an abundance of help available.

Pleasure ... or Problem?

You need to objectively review your drinking habits (*without* demonizing yourself) to determine if alcohol is a pleasurable indulgence, or an agent that you are using to either numb your pain or avoid grief altogether. Ask yourself the following (and be honest with yourself):

✓ Has your drinking increased dramatically since the loss of your spouse?
✓ Do you feel guilty about drinking?
✓ Do you attempt to hide your drinking (i.e., hiding bottles, covering up drinking with breath mints, etc.)?
✓ Do you need a drink before going to work or facing a social situation "just to get through?"

✓ Are you drinking directly out of loneliness and/or to lessen the pain of loss?

If you are answering yes to all or most of these questions, please check the resources in the back of this book to locate the help and support that you need (most of which is free of charge).

Make the World Go Away: Drug Abuse

It is now both widely known and understood that drug abuse does not refer to only the illicit. Drug abuse can also encompass prescription and over-the-counter medications. The problems arise when these medications are used outside of a doctor's close supervision.

When it comes to issues most associated with grief (depression, anxiety, etc.), a closely supervised regimen of medication can be incredibly beneficial, and once a diagnosis is confirmed,[2] these issues can be highly treatable. However, we also know that simply because a medication is either prescribed by a physician or mental health professional, or is as easily available as body wash and nail polish at the drugstore, it does not mean that these medications can't be dangerously misused or abused—and the results can be devastating.

There's a Pill for That

I remember the days when the only drugs that were advertised on television were over-the-counter headache remedies (remember

---

2 By a medical professional—not by the Internet and certainly not by yourself.

the Excedrin Headache?), stomach remedies (who could forget Alka-Seltzer's catchy, "Plop plop, fizz fizz, oh what a relief it is!"), and Bactine for cuts and scrapes ("Helps the hurt stop hurting" and bonus, it didn't sting!).[3] Nowadays, and owing to the legalization of prescription drug commercials in 1983, a cornucopia of various drugs are offered up as a nightly banquet on our airwaves. In short, it seems like there is an answer for every symptom in the world that can be suffered—and that answer is apparently in pill form.

That said, too many of us have gotten into our heads that it is a sign of weakness to try to cope with grief and bereavement by ourselves—and that is simply not true. Do I believe in the adage "A pill for everything and everything has a pill"? No. Do I believe that mental health issues are every bit as medically treatable as a sore throat or broken arm, and should be attended to with the same level of attention and respect? Most definitely.

Reaching Out for Help

Signs that prescription and/or over-the-counter drug use has become a problem include the following:

✓ Panicking if/when a medication runs out and/or making off-hour, non-emergency runs to the store to obtain more of the medication.

✓ Using strictly controlled medication without a physician's close supervision.

✓ Increasing and/or exceeding the indicated dosage.

✓ Visiting multiple doctors for the same or similar condition for the sole purpose of obtaining prescriptions.

---

3 I have just seriously dated myself.

✓ Consumption of over-the-counter drugs for the same conditions for which a doctor has already prescribed other medication.

Recreational (Illicit) Drugs

It seems silly to have to even discuss the myriad dangers of using illicit drugs. However, there are those who turn to these particular drugs as a method of coping with grief. These drugs are not in place to correct a chemical imbalance, battle depression, or relieve anxiety. These drugs serve only one purpose and that is to create an anesthetic effect or "high" of some sort. Whether the drug of choice provides a temporary sense of energy and euphoria, or an equally temporary sense of escape, numbness and "nothingness," what these drugs do *not* do is help you cope with grief, eliminate your problems, correct medical issues, or do much of anything other than endanger your health, your welfare, your relationships with family and loved ones, your bank account, your career, and your overall well-being. Even more tragic is the fact that many who abuse these drugs often do so in tandem with alcohol—a potentially lethal decision.

If you are currently using *any* illicit drug to cope with your grief, I strongly encourage you to avail yourself of the resources provided in the back of the book. There really is a healthy way through, and there are many people who stand ready to help you find your way.

Disordered Eating

There once was a time that the answers to eating issues consisted of such sage advice as, "You just need to lose weight" (for the overweight), or, "Why don't you just eat something" (to the under-weight). The good news is that disordered eating is now rightly recognized as a mental health issue and is being treated accordingly. The not-so-good news is that along with other manner of mental illness, disordered eating still carries a stigma that results in too many of its sufferers refusing to seek help and/or the people surrounding the sufferers continuing to say things like, "You just need to lose weight," or, "Why don't you just eat something?"[4]

The Relationship Between Food and Grief

The answers to the very complicated issue of disordered eating and grief are relatively simple. First, food is readily accessible. Food is not illegal.[5] Food doesn't require a prescription, and a great deal of food (especially in junk form) is relatively inexpensive. Second, and more to the point, in a life-and-death, loss-and-bereavement situation, where someone's world has just been catapulted into turmoil, the one thing that *is* controllable . . . is food. Whether they are restricting or bingeing, the person suffering from an eating disorder can actually feel a distorted sense of peace and calm in an otherwise chaotic situation through their unhealthy control of food.

Compliments Create Complications

"I developed anorexia and bulimia . . . because the thinner
you are, the more celebrated you are."

—Renee Peters, model

---

4 Which is rather like telling someone with a broken leg, *"Why don't you just get up and walk?"*

5 In other words, no one ever got pulled over by law enforcement for either eating too much or for eating too little.

Thanks in large part to the thousands of magazines, billboards, television shows, red-carpet critics, social media, and beauty experts (both legitimate and self-declared), body image has become an issue of gigantic proportion, creating an alleged "ideal" that few of us have any hope of achieving. Yet most of us have felt the pressure to look like the impossibly airbrushed visions by which we are greeted in what feels like every direction in which we turn. Many of us have tried at least one high fat/low fat, high carb/low carb, high protein/ low protein shake, pre-packaged meal, fancy-named fasting, cleansing, detoxing diet.[6] Now, what happens when you lose weight? Most likely, people around you will remark on how great you look—and who doesn't want to hear *those* magic words? Your wardrobe choices expand as your waistline shrinks. You feel attractive, dynamic, and perhaps for the first time in a long time—you feel in control.

Is there anything wrong with weight loss? When pursued in a healthy, doctor-approved manner, accompanied by both a predetermined plan and an end point, of course not. However, when used as a method of gaining control over grief or as a numbing agent against grief, weight loss can be carried to an extreme. For example:

- ✓ Saying to yourself, "*Just 'x' more pounds and then I'll stop,*" when weight loss is unnecessary.
- ✓ Emergence of adverse physical symptoms (loss of menstruation unrelated to menopause or peri-menopause, dizziness/ fainting, irregular heartbeat, etc.).
- ✓ Refusing to eat or self-inducing vomiting when you do eat.
- ✓ Dressing in layers to hide weight loss or to stay warm as you lose body fat.

---

6 If you could see me right now, you would see me sheepishly raising my hand.

✓ Preoccupation with weight, food, calories, and dieting.

✓ Restricting or eliminating entire food categories.

✓ Making frequent comments about feeling overweight, despite weight loss.

The Opposite End of the Spectrum

"'Fat' has become not a description of size, but a moral category tainted with criticism and contempt."

—Susie Orbach, psychotherapist and author

Being overweight has become the last "acceptable" prejudice that we have somehow permitted to exist in our society. It has been proven over and over again that those who are overweight are more likely to experience discrimination in the workplace and scorn, judgment, and ridicule in public places.

Absent a clinically diagnosed physical condition or certain medications that can cause weight gain, the matter of gaining weight is generally mathematical. When we consume more calories than we burn, the extra calories are stored as fat. When one is already consumed with grief, worrying about consuming too many calories is not usually a priority. Additionally, another aspect of grief is the realization that there is one less mouth at the dinner table–and fast food (either drive-through or prepackaged) can quickly become a staple of a widowed's diet.[7]

Whether food is used as a substitute for lost companionship or as a numbing agent against loss, binge eating can quickly become a destructive behavior. The hallmarks of binge eating include the following:

---

7 Sheepishly raising my hand once again.

✓ A feeling of no control over eating (the inability to stop eating once started).

✓ Eating until feeling uncomfortably full or to the point of physical pain.

✓ Eating large amounts of food when not feeling physically hungry.

✓ Eating alone because of embarrassment about how much one is eating, or hiding one's eating altogether.

✓ Feeling disgusted, depressed, and/or guilty after the bingeing episode.

Getting to the Heart of Handling Food

If you recognize yourself in these disorders, you are far from alone; in fact, sufferers number in the millions.[8] Experts who specialize in the diagnosis and treatment of eating disorders can help you determine if you are using food to cope with grief in an unhealthy way. Please do not hesitate to reach out for help, beginning with the resources in the back of the book.

"I'm a 'Shopaholic'"

An obvious riff on the words *alcoholic* and *workaholic*, the word *shopaholic* has become a cute, pop culture reference, emblazoned on T-shirts and shopping bags and used as a bragging point for those who (like myself) love to shop. However, a love of shopping can quickly devolve into a knee-jerk reaction, a balm with which to soothe wounds of all manner, including grief. It's also a potentially

---

8 Source: The National Association of Anorexia Nervosa and Associated Disorders (ANAD).

destructive coping avenue that can jeopardize or altogether anni-
hilate present and future financial security for years to come.

Why Do We Shop?

Obviously, there are things for which we must shop—food,
household goods, clothing, and other necessities. However, if these
were the only reasons that we went shopping, no store in the world
could sustain a truly profitable business. When it comes down to
it, there are basically two reasons that many of us shop: shopping
usually makes us feels *good*—and, particularly if we are really sad
or really mad, shopping makes us feel *better.*

Many years ago, I was unceremoniously dumped (in an e-mail,
no less) by a formerly ardent suitor. You know the type—he sent
flowers before we had gone on our first date, which was followed
by lovely dinners and outings, beautiful gifts for my birthday, and
constant compliments and commentary on my "perfection" as a
woman.[9] One day, and completely out of nowhere, I received an
e-mail from him, announcing that he'd had a "change of heart
upon re-examination of my life" and decided that my previously
perceived and vocally declared "perfection" ... wasn't. To be clear, I
was not in love with this person, but I was nevertheless willing to
give time to this new relationship—and was subsequently dropped
on my head. Out of nowhere. In an *e-mail.*

Furious, I grabbed my purse, headed immediately to the mall,
stormed into one of my favorite "athleisure" stores, and unloaded
all of my fury into their cash register—or at least as much fury as
my credit card budget would allow.

---

9 His words, not mine. I promise.

I freely admit to periodic "emotional shopping," and not just out of anger. Celebration, consolation, a reward for achieving a goal, and yes, in the midst of grieving—these were all justifiable reasons for a "retail therapy" excursion. However, the one thing that I have always been able to do with regard to shopping . . . is *stop*. I am acutely aware of my monthly budget and more importantly, I am acutely aware of my monthly responsibilities and obligations, both of which will always take priority over a perceived need to shop.

Out-of-Control Shopping

When shopping takes a toll on one's overall quality of life, finances, and/or relationships, it ceases to be cute and becomes a serious issue. Signs that you may be approaching a danger point include, but are not limited to the following:

- ✓ The inability to distinguish *want* from *need*
- ✓ Feeling guilt, self-loathing, or anxiety after a shopping trip
- ✓ Buying items that are never used
- ✓ Incurring a large amount of credit card debt
- ✓ Endangering financial obligation (missing mortgage or rent payments, car payments, utility payments, etc.) and/or incurring collections, judgments, liens, etc. as a direct result of shopping habits

If you see yourself in any of these categories, please seek the help of an expert who specializes in this particular disorder.

"I'm So Lonely": Getting (Overly) Physical

One of my earliest forays into the world of, "Are you really going to talk about *that?*" addressed the issues surrounding (*gasp!*)

post-widowhood intimacy.[10] On its face, sexual bereavement may sound frivolous; almost as if the loss emphasis should be strictly on the emotional aspect. However, sex is so much more than the wrinkling of bedsheets that many envision when the subject is broached. Sex is also about a true intimacy that has been ripped away—and there is an obvious emotional component to intimacy as well. Stolen glances and knowing smiles across a room.[11] Feeling both desired and desirable. Knowing that even when surrounded by crowds of people, you are a couple. You are that brand of "special" to one person, and they are, in turn, that same level of "special" to you, too.

Oh yeah... we do miss wrinkling bedsheets, too—a feeling that, despite time, age, grief, or any other set of circumstances, rarely disappears.

Mr./Ms. Right vs. Mr./Ms. Right Now (or "Let's Just Get It Over With")

Over the years, a number of widows have mustered the courage to ask about engaging in sex just for the sake of having sex:[12]

- ✓ "What if you're 'physically' ready for a relationship but not emotionally?"
- ✓ "Do you think you can just have sex without the 'complications' of a relationship?"
- ✓ "I've been tempted to just 'get it over with,' and I'm wondering if that's a good idea."

---

10 Yes, believe it or not, the widowed actually do miss sex and yearn for physical connection—and it is okay to feel that way.

11 In a genuine way, not in a phony, corny-erectile-dysfunction-commercial kind of way.

12 Yes, it *does* take courage to ask the question when you are terrified of both the answer and what people will think of you for asking the question to begin with.

Get it "over with?" Are we talking about undergoing root canal? Sex and intimacy is supposed to be a beautiful experience between two people, not something to "get over with," or otherwise approach with the same attitude as you might have at the thought of undergoing a tax audit.

As much as we might wish it were otherwise and despite what certain magazines and saucy television shows may tell us, most people cannot separate physical and emotional intimacy. In an interview that I gave to *The New York Times*,[13] I shared (in pertinent part):

> "When you're missing physical connection with another person, you can make decisions that are not always in your best interest. Sex can cloud one's judgment. It helps to take sex out of the equation and reassess a relationship before becoming sexually intimate."

I personally liken "sex for the sake of sex" to taking the time to do fabulous hair and makeup on yourself and getting all dressed up to go out, but rather than enjoying steak and champagne, you instead head to a convenience store for a can of Pringles and a Diet Coke. It may taste okay, it might even momentarily take away your hunger, but it is not exactly what you would call deliciously satisfying.

Although you may intellectually believe that your needs are strictly limited to the physical, in reality, what you are truly longing for is *closeness;* something that takes emotional involvement. If you are not ready emotionally and you choose to get involved with someone physically, you're likely to wind up feeling pretty empty

---

13 Excerpt: "*When a Partner Dies: Grieving the Loss of Sex,*" by Jane Brody; *The New York Times,* March 7, 2017.

after the fact. I know that a lack of physical connectivity is diffi-cult; however, if you are willing to wait for what you really want, *and* you are willing to wait until you are ready in all respects, it is *so* worth it.

When Desire Becomes Dangerous: Sexual Compulsiveness

You now know that sexual bereavement is a real thing. However (and sadly), there are those who are affected by sexual bereave-ment to the point that they may carry physical engagement to a dangerous extreme. When it comes to the widowed community, sexually compulsive activity is generally a result of depression, anxiety, stress, and/or, of course, grief and loneliness. A sufferer can be so in need of filling the void left by their beloved that they go in search of a "substitute," if you will. Unfortunately, the void is filled only momentarily and very superficially. When it is time to bid good-bye to Mr./Ms. Right Now, odds are that they may never again see their temporary void-filler.[14] When they once again feel the void and that longing and loneliness, the cycle resumes.

What makes matters both worse and more dangerous is that the longer the cycle continues, the less attention is paid to caution. Axioms such as "Know your partner" and "Use a condom" tend to go out the window when the only concern is with sexual satisfac-tion—not to mention the scary possibilities of inviting the wrong person into your intimate space. In a compulsive moment, cautions and caveats are easily tossed to the wind in favor of satisfying the compulsion.

---

14 In all fairness, a sufferer may not *want* to see that person again.

Symptoms of sexual compulsion include, but are not limited to:

✓ Sexual impulses that you feel are beyond your control
✓ You do not find actual sexual activity satisfying
✓ Using sex as a way to avoid the grieving process or as an escape from loneliness, depression, or anxiety
✓ Continuing to engage in sexual behaviors that may have serious consequences (getting or giving someone a sexually transmitted disease, putting your personal safety at risk, etc.)
✓ Little or no desire to establish a close, committed relationship

If you are battling sexual compulsivity, or if you are tempted toward sexual compulsivity, don't hesitate to seek help from those in a position to help you. You have no reason to feel shame, embarrassment, or guilt—experts in this field are trained to help you confront the compulsion and will do so without casting judgment.

A Tragically Permanent Solution: Suicide

"How selfish."
"They had everything to live for . . ."
"He/She was so handsome/pretty/well-off . . ."
"Why would they do that to their family?"

These are some of the most common responses when people learn that someone has committed suicide. Far too many people either do not understand or don't care to understand what is going through the mind of a suicidal person—and to proffer disparaging opinions on suicide (or its victims) is, at best, insensitive and unsympathetic. At worst, it is dangerous.

What Causes a Person to Resort to Suicide?

The reasons behind resorting to suicide are as varied as there are people who lose their lives to suicide. However, one of the common denominators that suicide victims share is that they are in so much pain (physical, mental, emotional, or a combination thereof) that they do not see a way through. They oftentimes feel burdensome to people around them. They don't want to feel "better;" rather, they simply do not wish to feel at all. The fact that they are pretty or handsome or well-off or "have everything going for them" is immaterial, because if someone is *that* depressed and in *that* much pain, all of the "everything going for them" in the world is completely irrelevant.

To the Survivors of a Loved One's Suicide

On a personal note, my own family experienced the suicidal deaths of two relatives within three years. It is a horrendous experience through which to live and one that leaves its survivors with nothing but questions, some of which may never be answered.

Professionally, I have worked with and spoken before many widowed whose spouses died as a result of suicide. Some survivors bristle when I speak in reference to the fact that our spouses did not choose to leave our marriages[15]—the rationale being that widowed survivors' spouses "chose" suicide, hence they "chose" to leave the marriage—leaving the surviving spouse laden with the heavy burden of guilt.

---

15 As opposed to divorce, where somebody somewhere made a conscious choice to leave the marriage.

I fervently believe that even though their deaths were by their own hand, people who die by suicide don't choose to leave, either their marriages or this world. Victims of suicide are in overwhelming pain; a pain masked by a rationale that we cannot understand. They see no way around or through that personal pain. In other words, it's not that they chose to leave or that they even *wanted* to leave . . . they felt that there was no way for them to stay.

Suicide Is Not the Solution

You have lost your spouse. The pain is overwhelming and you've never felt more alone. You have no idea what to do first, or next . . . or for the foreseeable future. The swirling of emotions in your head and in your heart is almost too much to bear. You don't care to be engaged with life, because along with the end of your spouse's life, the life that you knew with them has come to an end, too.

Though I do not have all the answers to all of life's questions, this much I know with absolute certainty: suicide is not now, nor will it ever be, the answer to any life challenge. Suicide is a tragically permanent solution to what is a temporary situation, no matter how horrifically painful. Now, by "temporary situation," I obviously do not mean loss or grief. You'll learn in your next Bereavement Boot Camp lesson that grief never truly leaves us. However, as you move through your grief, the *form* that grief takes shifts and changes complexion. In other words, today is indeed not forever.

When you seek the help that you need (both with how you are feeling right now and how you are going to face and deal with the future), it truly *does* get better—a fact to which millions of us will attest.

Recognizing the Signs

Signs that someone is in imminent danger of resorting to suicide include:

✓ Talking about wanting to die or to kill oneself.
✓ Looking for a way to kill oneself, such as researching methodologies online or obtaining a gun.
✓ Talking about feeling hopeless or having no reason to live.

Please immediately contact the National Suicide Prevention Lifeline at 800-273-TALK (8255) or 911 without delay. The NSPL also has a twenty-four-hour live online chat option; additional information is listed in the back of the book.

According to the Suicide Resource Prevention Center,[16] signs that someone may be contemplating or planning suicide include:

✓ Talking about being in unbearable pain.
✓ Talking about being a burden to others.
✓ Increasing the use of alcohol or drugs (or other destructive behaviors).
✓ Withdrawing or isolating.
✓ Disposing of personal belongings for no apparent reason.
✓ Displaying extreme mood swings.[17]

The NSPL stands ready twenty-four hours a day, seven days a week to help those in immediate crisis. You have *nothing* of which to be afraid or ashamed. They will help you get through this horrible season in time, and direct you toward the help that you need.

---

16 Source: The Suicide Prevention Resource Center *www.sprc.org*.

17 Keep in mind that someone who has "made peace" with a decision to commit suicide may exhibit an outwardly unusual level of happiness or high-energy behavior during a time of bereavement.

You know how I keep saying that there is no shame in seeking help? That statement has never been more true than right this minute.

Please don't let despair determine your destiny. The feeling of despair is momentary and those feelings can be worked through and resolved. Allow in the help. Allow in the light. Together, we can get you through this.

The One Common Denominator

The one common denominator that runs through much of what we have discussed in this chapter is that while destructive coping mechanisms all, these behaviors are *treatable*. They are *correctable* and, in the case of suicidal ideation, they are *preventable*. *Please* consult the resources provided in this book. *Please* recognize that what and how you are feeling is real, it is legitimate, and, if you are coping with your grief in a destructive manner, it is fixable.

Most of all, please never, ever cease to remind yourself that *you are not alone.* There is help. There is hope. There is promise. There is indeed life after loss.

EKITA!

Are you listening to too many other people telling you how your
healing journey ought to be, what it should look like,
or where it should take you?
Are you very busy striving for perfection based on
other people's opinions?
Are you striving for perfection based upon
your *own* expectations?

♥

Quit wasting your time and energy.
Quit discouraging yourself.
Quit beating up on yourself.
Quit trying to please everyone around you.
Quit striving for an "ideal" healing journey,
because that ideal doesn't exist.

♥

Most importantly, *please* quit trying to mold yourself and/or your
healing journey into what others think it (or you) should be—
no matter *who* those other people are.

♥

Strive instead for *your own* brand of excellence.
Design *your own* healing journey.
Just be the very best *you* that you can be.
Today.
That's all you really ever have to do.

8

Bereavement Boot Camp Lesson Three: Stop Putting Off Proactivity

I n this lesson, we are going to take an honest look at how proactive you have *truly* been on your healing journey, regardless of when or how that journey began for you. Remember that as with any part of Boot Camp, this lesson will work only if you are honest with yourself.

Lest you think that you are being rushed through your healing processes, let's start with a very important reminder: Grieving is essential. It can't be circumvented. It can't be accomplished with a shortcut, click-through mentality. Grieving is a vital component of your healing process. Sharing insights on how to heal should never be confused with or taken as a message to "hurry up" or instructions on how to avoid the grieving process.

Yes, grief hurts—a lot. Grief is dark and lonely and sad and all things painful. However, rushing the process is never beneficial. Glossing over, attempting to distract yourself from or trying to avoid grief in any way (regardless of method[1]) will only result in that grief coming back to bite you, be it within a few months or many years later. You can't ignore, stuff down inside, keep busy through, or successfully sidetrack the reality that was and is your loss and the grieving process that must follow.

All of that understood, we also want to feel better—and we *should* want to feel better. We eventually want to actually *be* better. However, "better" does not happen by sitting around and waiting for it to magically show up. Better doesn't knock on your door and shout, "Here I am!" Better begins with a choice: a conscious decision to do what it takes to begin (or continue) healing in a productive way.

Years ago, I provided one-on-one peer coaching to widows. I once coached a widow who was almost two years along in her journey when she came to me. After listening to her story and after having seen her many posts on social media sharing how terrible she was feeling, I asked her what she had done to try to move herself forward on her healing journey:

What books had she read? *None.*
What audio or DVD help had she sought? *None.*
Support groups? *Didn't like them.*
Online support groups? *Not for her* (but she was nevertheless a
    willing participant in social media).
Any print or web articles that she found helpful? *No.*
Did she even *look* for any helpful print or web articles? *Not really.*

---

1 Work, children and their activities, major projects, etc.

Admittedly puzzled, I asked her why she had not availed herself of any tools at all that might contribute to moving her forward on her healing journey. She replied that since "time is supposed to heal all wounds," she was waiting until "enough time has passed"[2] and at that point, she figured that she would automatically feel better. Not a great strategy, folks.

Let's first review the whole "Time heals all wounds" nonsense (and if you've ever heard me speak or teach, or read anything I've written, consider this a refresher). After your loss, has anyone ever said to you: "Time heals all wounds?" If you've ever heard this ridiculous cliché (and most of you have heard it at least once), did you want to hit something hard and scream *"When?!"*

I have some unfortunate news for you: time *alone* cannot, does not, and will not "heal all wounds."

Think about this: When a surgeon operates, do they make an incision, conduct the surgery, and then just walk away from the operating table saying, "Time will heal this wound?" Of course not. A surgeon uses appropriate tools to complete the surgery. They follow up on the healing process. Eventually, with proper tools, attention, care, *and* time, the surgical wound heals, likely leaving a scar.

Now, let's look at your loss the same way. Are you truly just waiting for time to heal your loss-wound? Are you waking up every day, thinking, *"Well, time has passed and everyone is telling me that time heals all wounds, but I don't feel 'healed'—what's the matter with me?"*

If you are simply waiting for time to heal your wound, the only thing that you are going to accomplish is a whole lot of waiting.

---

2 For the record, I have never found the word "enough" on any clock or calendar.

The fact is that time alone can't be the only factor in your healing process. Just like a surgeon, you need tools and you need to get your hands on every single tool available. When it comes to your loss, have you used any tools: books (aside from this one), magazines, audio aids, seminars, the Internet, individual counseling, or coaching, support groups—anything and everything to get you on the road to recovery? If your answer is no, then you are the patient on that operating table with a wide-open wound that time alone *cannot and will not heal.*

If you have utilized various tools and those tools didn't accomplish what you expected or needed, get more tools! Everyone receives their particular brain and heart messages of comfort, support, and education in different ways. Therefore, it follows that the grief education that helped one person may not necessarily speak to you in the ways that you require. If a certain grief recovery tool or approach does not work for you, that's completely fine. However, it does not automatically mean that *all* grief recovery strategies won't work for you. Just because one book (or two, or five, or eight) did not help you, it doesn't mean that the next book won't help. Just because one support group or online community or therapist was not a good fit, it doesn't mean you should stop looking for a group or community or therapist who might be a perfect fit.

It's time to take that honest look at yourself. What specific steps have you taken to move yourself forward? Are you truly being proactive on your healing journey in every way possible . . . or are you simply waiting for the passage of time to heal everything? If any one of your answers to these questions were in the negative, it is time to get whatever tools you need to continue creating *your* healing journey, the tools that are really going to speak to you and take you in the direction that you wish to go. Get proactive, get serious, and start caring properly for the loss-wound you have sustained. When you have the right tools, when you attend to and care for that loss-wound that will eventually turn into a life scar, *that's* when time begins to help the wound—and *you*—heal.

The "Fog" that Furthers the Pain

Here's another reason why this whole "time heals all wounds" nonsense doesn't hold water. The times are countless when I have heard, "You know, Carole, the first year was really hard but the second [or subsequent] year was even worse. It seems like the longer they're gone, the more you miss them." This sentiment is more common than you may realize.

Think about this for a moment. Have you ever had any major dental work? When you do, the dentist generally uses some kind of anesthetic to allow drilling or pounding or extracting or other really pleasant stuff. What happens after the dentist is finished drilling or pounding or extracting and that anesthetic wears off in a few hours? It hurts—a *lot*.

Now, let's look at time passing after loss the same way. One of the main reasons that you may actually feel worse as time passes is that the "grief fog"—the emotional anesthetic that cushions us against the shock of our losses—begins to wear off. The grief fog begins to lift and the pain becomes sharper, more acute, and more real. So instead of feeling better with the passing of time (as so many people who surround the bereaved expect and, sadly, sometimes even demand), you can actually feel *worse*.

Grief Delayed Is Grief Denied

Yet another reason you may be feeling the pain even more intensely as time passes is that you may have not allowed yourself adequate time to heal immediately post-loss. There is no shame in that of course, but as my mother used to tell me, "If you skip over any part of your life, at some point in time, you will go back to retrieve it." So, for whatever reasons—someone told you that you should be "over it;" someone caused you to do what I call "believe and bury," where you believe another person's thoughts, feelings, or opinions and buried your feelings as a result; you busied your-self with work, children, or other activities; or maybe you were estranged from your late spouse and felt that you weren't entitled to grieve—whatever the case, at the time of your loss and in the weeks, months, or years since, you were not permitted to truly grieve. Now, you are rectifying the grief delay by retrieving and dealing with that part of your healing journey. . . . That's a *good* thing. It is a *positive* thing.

Your Time Zone

The primary reason that time doesn't heal all wounds is that your "loss clock" functions a bit differently from everyone else. For anyone who has suffered this level of loss, time stops at the moment of the loss. The life that you knew stops. The world that you knew stops. The anticipation of the future that you had planned *stops*. It takes a whole lot of time to even figure out how to restart your life clock again, since everything you once knew has been turned upside down.

However, even though your clock has momentarily stopped, everyone else's clock keeps right on ticking along. Time is passing for everyone else but you, because your life clock stopped at the moment that your world stopped. How then can *anyone* say that "time heals all wounds" when your time frames involve completely different time zones?[3]

In sum, does time heal all wounds? No.

Your time, based on *your* life clock, plus the tools that *you* choose, can combine and coalesce and help with turning a loss wound into a life scar over time. Time can temper and shift the rawness and intensity of the pain of loss. Time can alter the shape and complexion of loss, but the loss is always there. The grief is always a part of you. It never goes away. It changes shape, form, and feature, but it never entirely disappears.

Think about this for a second. Envision anything that is exposed to nature—mountains, boulders and rock formations, sand dunes (a typical Californian observation to make), even Mount Rushmore. Think about what happens to these things over time. Wind shifts formations. Rain and snow alter shape, appearance, and textures … but the mountain remains. The boulders and rock formations remain. Even the sand dunes are still there. The same can be said about your loss. Time shifts the intensity, the shape, and complexion of loss, but the loss itself will *always* be there. In other words, a *healed* wound does not mean a *disappearing* wound.

Here is your third Boot Camp Affirmation. Keep it in front of you.

---

3 Do you see how I have punched holes in this "time healing wounds" thing? You can too.

I recognize that merely allowing time to pass will not further my healing journey. I also recognize that I can't avoid the grieving process, and attempts to so will only result in my grief eventually resurfacing. I will therefore commit to being proactive (or *more* proactive) on my journey, beginning with the acquisition of any and all healing tools that speak to me in a positive and inspirational way. I also recognize that support surrounds me. I will avail myself of the support of others who understand exactly what I have been through, whether it is through an in-person support group or an online support community. Lastly, if I have made a sincere effort to move forward and I still don't feel as though I'm making progress, I will consult with my doctor, my cleric, a coach, a therapist, a mental health expert, or anyone else who is in a position to help.

Boot Camp Challenge

List absolutely everything that you've done to move yourself forward on your healing journey—and that means *everything*. List all of the books, articles, groups, coaching, therapies, retreats, conferences, and other means of support that you have acquired and/or utilized. Now carefully review the list. What helped? What didn't help? What is helping you right now? What is not really doing much good? Write it down next to the item(s) on your list. Put a star by what has helped or is currently helping you, and either discard or make alterations to the item(s) that you do not feel are helping you thrive.

Don't have a list? Not to worry—your list is beginning right now. Your challenge is to acquire just one *new* tool within the next week to either begin or add to your toolkit. You might consider something that you have not done before or that you've thought about but haven't done yet. Perhaps it's linking up with an online community of support or joining a support group in your area. Maybe it's acquiring a new book or other learning tool that you have not yet tried, or signing up for a retreat or conference. Whatever you decide, add *one* new tool to your healing journey—and then *use* it.

List of all tools that I've used on my healing journey up to this point.

1. _____
2. _____
3. _____
4. _____
5. _____
6. _____
7. _____
8. _____
9. _____
10. _____

The one new tool that I wish to add is: _____

Additional tools I'd like to add include:

1. _____
2. _____
3. _____
4. _____
5. _____
6. _____

How I feel after acquiring my new tool(s): _____

_____
_____
_____
_____
_____
_____

EKITA!

Whether it's:

Having a moment of tears,

Having a moment of laughter,

Deciding to date again,

Deciding not to date again,

Deciding not to date again . . . yet.

Making decisions about your rings,

No matter *what* those decisions may be,

Selling your home,

Staying in your home,

Or even something as simple as

treating yourself to something lovely . . .

Do you find yourself now or have you ever found yourself

apologizing to others

for how you're handling any part

or all of your healing journey?

❤

If so, you need to stop.

Right now.

❤

There is nothing regarding your healing journey

for which you need to apologize or feel guilty.

Not. One. Thing.

Embrace this important concept as you continue healing.

Attack of the Grief Monster

There is a monster that quietly lurks among those who are bereaved. It is stealthy and sneaky and pounces when we both most *and* least expect it. As with most monsters, this one, too, appears in the quiet and lonely of night. However, this particular monster can strike during the daytime hours as well. It attacks randomly, even in the most mundane of moments and without any care for its victims. It attacks during what are supposedly fun or happy times, and most definitely makes an appearance during frustrating or challenging times. It chooses its attack moments very carefully. A song, a food, a scent, a place, a date on the calendar, even a particular time of day is ready invitation. The impact? Overwhelming sadness, tears, depression, and generally feeling as though your loss happened just five minutes ago.

Who is this beast? It's the Grief Monster, and when it attacks, it has the capability of stalling—or even halting—a healing journey in its tracks, as though a person is back at square one.

❦

About three months after Mike's death, I was at the mall to purchase a birthday gift. As I lazily meandered through the maze of department store cosmetic and perfume counters, the Grief Monster struck quite suddenly and very hard. Speaking frankly, the Grief Monster grabbed me around my throat and kicked my knees out from under me. How? While browsing those lovely counters, I had inadvertently caught a whiff of Mike's cologne—his fragrant calling card. His invisible yet indelible signature. The one without which he never left the house. The one that sweetly lingered in the air after he left for work. The one that always let us know that he was "there," even if he wasn't at home. The one that I sprayed on my pillow after he passed away.

My insides turned to Jell-O. Caught completely by surprise and feeling the simultaneous burn and sting of overflowing tears and the familiar hint of post-loss nausea, I bolted from the store, ran for my car, sped to the sanctuary of home, and sobbed in the darkness for hours afterward.

The Grief Monster. We naturally expect it to show up at night, when all is quiet—and it usually does not disappoint. We all but set a place for it on birthdays, on holidays or when other celebratory milestone events occur. However, and as we all know, the Grief Monster can also strike at inopportune and seemingly innocuous times throughout our day. Worse, victims of a Grief Monster attack believe that because they're having a moment of sadness or tears or grief, regardless of the grief trigger involved, they believe themselves to be "backsliding" or otherwise having a setback on their healing journey.

It is simply not true.

When you take a road trip (and particularly if the state of California is involved in any way), the times are rare that you go from Point A to Point B without some kind of a hiccup. It could be a detour, a lane closure, or, at the very least, a traffic jam. However, any one or all of these obstacles do not usually result in your winding up back on your front doorstep. You likely don't throw up your hands and wail, "I'm right back to where I began this thing." Instead, you assess the obstacle in the moment and you make your way around it or through it. It requires a bit of time and patience; however, you still manage to find your way to your destination.

The exact same thing can be said for your healing journey. There will be bumps, detours, and "jams"—those times when you may feel as though you are standing still or even traveling backward. The problem with buying into this mindset is the implication that you are right back where you started, thereby negating any progress that you've made on your healing journey. You cannot punish yourself in this manner by trivializing or altogether dismissing the progress that you have made to this point. Regardless of whether you lost your beloved ten years or ten minutes ago, you have indeed progressed. You are slowly moving forward, you are pursuing healing, and as long as you continue to take baby steps forward, a setback is simply not possible.

The One Great Fear Among Widowed . . . and How to Overcome It

Most people are afraid of dying, which is not an unusual or irrational fear. However, many people are so afraid of it that they do not even want to discuss the subject. In too many cases, this particular fear can cause people to either postpone or outright refuse to make wills or carry life insurance (which is downright irresponsible)—and we have all likely heard at least one person refuse to attend a funeral, saying, "I don't like funerals,"[1] all out of a fear of the inevitable day when they will no longer be here on Earth.

Along with Grief Monster attacks, there exists another common fear in Widowed World: the fear of *living*. To those outside of Widowed World, this may sound completely absurd, perhaps almost comical. Who on *Earth* would be afraid of *life:* of getting up every day and going to sleep every night, of going to work or school, of picnics and paying bills, of kids' activities and holidays? The answer? The widowed.

Fear—of the future, of starting over from scratch, of being alone—is really dread for one thing, truly one of the greatest fears of them all: the unknown.

Catapulted into a life that was unplanned, unexpected, undesired, and is perhaps even right now unbearable, you may find yourself absolutely terrified of life. While necessary, leaving the house for work is nonetheless fraught with fear. Socializing is completely out of the question, and even answering the phone gives you cause for pause. What you may not be able to figure out is *why*.

Even more important than the "why" component of the fear of the unknown is the "how." *How* do you combat the fear of the unknown, this greatest fear of them all? *How* do you triumph over the fear of living that most widowed have experienced at some point on their healing journeys? *How* do you push past the fear and move forward into your new life?

Fight back.

---

1 As opposed to those of us who *like* funerals?

Hard.

Become fear's greatest foe.

The archenemies to fear of the unknown are:

✓ Proactivity
✓ Education
✓ Support
✓ Community

It's impossible for proactivity and fear to coexist in the same space. When you become truly proactive in your healing journey by surrounding yourself with the tools that you need—the education that is absolutely integral to your healing (including this book), the support that best speaks to you, and a community who understands and encourages your processes—you'll be propelled forward in a positive way, and the fear begins to slowly diminish. When you begin to take control over an area of your life where you may have had virtually no control, your confidence in you specifically and with living in general starts to resurface. When you begin to see the actual fruits of your proactivity—going out and genuinely enjoying yourself, learning or trying something new, making new friends, doing even something as simple as accomplishing a household task that was once your late spouse's responsibility—the fear continues to weaken and, little by little, eventually disappears.

It's very easy to tell someone, "Don't be afraid."[2] Here's a news flash: *Everyone* in the widowed community has been afraid at some point. *All* widowed everywhere know and comprehend the fear of the unknown and, at one time or another, most have been

---

2 Especially when the person saying this may not have experienced being widowed and may not be afraid of anything at the moment.

absolutely paralyzed by that same fear. Understand that it's okay to be afraid, as long as you also understand that this fear does not get to take over and rule your life. While it is true that we can't control the circumstances that have taken our spouses away, we can certainly control our *reactions* to loss and chart the course that we want to take in our healing. The fact is that life is not meant to be feared. Life is meant to be treasured and savored and lived as loudly, largely, and lovingly as possible.

Remember one more thing: the definition of courage isn't "not being afraid." The definition of true courage is being afraid, and holding your head up high, taking a deep breath—and moving forward anyway.

Seven years after Mike's death, I was at the National Cheerleading Championships in Las Vegas to watch Kendall compete. When her team was announced as National Champions in their division and subsequent adolescent-cheerleader pandemonium loudly reigned, I began to softly cry. But this time, my tears weren't in a reaction to a Grief Monster attack. This time, the tears felt different—because those tears *were* different.

As the aforesaid pandemonium continued, I took a moment, looked toward the sky, gave two thumbs upward and, through the tears, quietly said, "She did it, Fleet," before wiping the tears away and quickly returning to the celebration at hand. Even though I was again feeling Mike's absence acutely, that brief moment nonetheless felt warm and peaceful, not at all like that horrible Grief Monster with whom I had wrestled so many times over the years that Mike had been gone.

I then realized that throughout the healing journey of the previous years and in the ensuing years since, the Grief Monster had gently transformed into sort of a "Fond Moments Fairy"—a gentle, guiding presence that will remain with me for the rest of my life. The same things that used to whip my emotions into a hurricane of Category Five proportions had eventually become both fond moments and tender memories that make me smile and feel a sense of peace, even if the smiles and laughter are occasionally through tears.

Sadness, crying, anger, grieving, moments of quiet, even a full-on Grief Monster assault does *not* equal "setback" or "backsliding." It's a moment. It's a hitch. It's that brief bump, detour, or jam on your healing journey. Embrace that monster, along with whatever emotion(s) that the monster is bringing out in you at that moment —and then let the monster go and continue forward. You have *not* backslid to the beginning. You have *not* had a setback that negates all that you've accomplished. You are simply finding your way through the detour.

Best of all, your Grief Monster is transforming. It's becoming a Fond Moments Fairy. It's becoming smiles through tears. It's becoming remembrance through rough times. It's becoming your peace.

EKITA!

You may not feel brave or strong twenty-four hours a day
. . . and that's understandable.
In fact, many bereaved become quite angry
when they are constantly told how brave or strong they are,
and that is understandable too.

❤

But even during moments of what you may
perceive to be weakness,
Don't lose sight of a very clear and positive choice
that you've made.

❤

For you have chosen healing.

❤

Perhaps without even realizing it,
you've decided that your emphasis will
continue to be on healing
and allowing others to support you
on your healing journey.
Just by letting others in,
Giving glimpses into your heartbreaking experiences,
allowing others' experiences into your heart,

giving advice to others,
heeding the suggestions of others,
finding your way.

❤

And even on the not-so-strong days,
even on the not-so-brave days,
even on the I-honestly-don't-give-a-damn days,
even on the I-just-can't-do-this-anymore days,
you have still chosen a path of healing.
You've chosen *your* path of healing . . .
and that's something of which to be very proud indeed.

CHAPTER
10

Are You Grieving "Right"? What's "Right," What's "Wrong"...and WTF?

A s you've likely surmised by now, I've always taken great umbrage with those who criticize, question, or issue judgment as to how the widowed handle their grief and their highly individual and intensely personal healing journeys. Unfortunately, there seems to be a lot of this sort of behavior—and worse yet, it's causing amazing people who are going through one of the worst experiences that they will ever know to actually question their feelings, their journeys, their judgment, their hearts—and themselves.

For example, a widow in New York shared the following:

> I need to know if I'm a bad person. My mother-in-law is constantly asking if I've been to the cemetery. I don't think of [my

husband as] being there. I want to think of him out hunting in the woods or fishing on the bank. [My mother-in-law] makes me feel like I don't care. Am I bad to feel this way? She and I are not grieving the same way and maybe I'm not doing it right.

Is she "bad"? Not "doing it right"? She's lost her husband and now she's being made to think of herself as bad and that somehow there's a "right" or "wrong" way to grieve.

We next hear from a widow in Wisconsin:

> I had taken my husband off of life support, which was the hardest thing for me to do. I had to listen to the doctors give bad news and no hope every time a test result came in. My mind was constantly on what was best for my husband. Now [my mother-in-law] is bringing things up about the choices I made, and saying that the doctors aren't truthful, and that I just let [the doctors] murder my husband. I've had our third baby and she is three months old. I also have a six-year-old and a three-year-old, and I'm just trying to hold it together.

Let's assess: Our widowed friend has a brand-new baby, two other little ones, has just lost her husband, and is being made to feel like she permitted the "murder" of her husband by medical personnel, all because she was a wife, acting in the position of advocate, who had to make a medical choice on her husband's behalf.

Thankfully, many widowed quickly jumped in to offer support and words of wisdom in response to these quandaries. A widow in New Hampshire states:

> I can relate where in-laws are questioning medical decisions. My in-laws took the medical records and sent them to an attorney to see

if there was any malpractice, which was not evident. They still hate the hospital and the doctors. The events surrounding his passing will forever remain a mystery to me; however, I can't continue to question myself.

Another widow in Virginia added:

I decided months ago to "run away" during the week of the [anniversary of my husband's] death. A few family members made unkind comments about my being on vacation on the anniversary. You know what? They can think what they want. Each of us processes grief differently and I have chosen to sit on a beach. There will be no unhappy reminders of "us" and that's how I want it.

And from a widow in New Jersey:

I've learned that the only way to grieve is to do it in your own way and in your own time. We honor our loved ones' memories in different ways, and only we know what's best for us.

What's the worst part in all of this? There are literally *millions* more stories just like these. They are stories of widowed who have lost their spouses and, on top of the loss, on top of the grief, and on top of the pain, they're being told things such as:[1]

✓ "You're not grieving right."
✓ "You killed him."
✓ "I'm ashamed you were married to her."
✓ "Why are you so upset? It's not like you were married or anything."

---

1 These are direct quotes.

And these are just a very few examples.

To *anyone* who has experienced anything remotely similar to what these widowed have shared, I would ask that you review and remember the wise words that have come directly from the widowed community—*your* widowed community:

> "I can't continue to question myself."
> "They can think what they want. It's about us and not them."
> "We honor our loved ones' memories in different ways and only we know what is best for us."

Never again should you question your right to grieve, mourn, and recover in the ways that you see fit; nor should you allow anyone else to question you. You are *finished* with judgment cast upon you by people who have no right to judge. You are *finished* questioning your decisions, your judgment, and your feelings. You are *finished* with the "coulda, shoulda, woulda" portion of the program that has become your new normal.

Always remember that when it comes to grief and loss recovery and the path that you choose to forge on your healing journey, there is no "right." There is no "wrong."[2] There is only *you*.

And whatever *you* decide is right for *you*—is right.

---

2 Coping with grief in a destructive manner is never acceptable. If you are finding it difficult to deal with your loss, your grief, or if you are coping in a destructive or potentially destructive manner, please refer to Chapter Seven ("When Grieving Becomes Dangerous...") and *immediately* seek the help of your doctor, cleric and/or mental health professional, along with the resources listed in the back of the book.

EKITA!

Sometimes, saying or doing what you believe
to be right and honest
will make you unpopular.
Sometimes, you'll elicit opinions from people
that are hurtful, spiteful, or vitriolic.
Sometimes, your motivations will be
unkindly questioned and cruelly slammed.
Sometimes, the people whom you believed would
always be there for you
choose instead to leave your life.
Sometimes, people claim unconditional love . . .
and then present you with a list of conditions.
Sometimes, you'll trust and believe in people
who say that they "have your back"
—and they don't.

♥

Sometimes, your faith—in a higher power, in life,
in people, and in yourself—
will be put to the test.
Sometimes, you'll call your healing journey into question.
Sometimes, people in your life

or the circumstances of your life
will knock you down—hard.
Sometimes, standing up for what and how
you believe is incredibly difficult.

❤

Stand up anyway.
Have the integrity and courage of your convictions.

❤

No one knows your heart as well as you do.
No one can take away your power, your voice, or your courage.
And always remember that *sometimes* isn't *always*.
Except for the fact that
those "sometimes" people described above
will *always* eventually go away.

CHAPTER
11

Don't Speak:
The Censorship of Grief

Whether it's in person or in writing, one of my most oft-repeated teachings is encouraging the bereaved to talk about their loss: their feelings and fears, their annoyances and anger, their uncertainties and unknowns. I firmly believe that continuing to express oneself throughout the grieving process (no matter how long that process may be) is a healthy, productive, and proactive way of coping.

However, and unfortunately, a bereaved person can inadvertently choose the wrong set of ears with which to share their deepest, most intimate feelings surrounding their loss. Even worse, they may not realize that this is the wrong person until that person makes the very insensitive attempt to censor them. Someone who is obviously in pain is looking for any number of things: solace, encouragement, strength, advice, hope ... or perhaps just someone to hold a hand, wipe away a tear, and gently say, "I'm here, and I understand."

The Shut Off and Shut Down

Susan recalls trying to talk about her late husband, only to be met by resistance from, of all people, *his* family. Susan shares:

His family continually asked me, "When are you going to get over it and get on with your life?" I was surprised when friends did the same thing. Some went through his entire illness with us, but after his death, they didn't want to even hear his name. They would tell me, "You talk about him too much; you need to get over it." When this happens you are numb and in shock. It's like being stabbed in the heart. Even after many years, it takes your breath away.

I have long taught that every person in the world can be categorized into one of two columns: Energy Givers and Energy Drainers. Energy Givers are fantastic. Energy Givers have attitudes that are wonderfully contagious. They are uplifting and positive, and are the people for whom you are (or will be) better for having spent time in their space. Energy Givers are not immune to bad days or problems of their own; they just choose not to lend more power to negativity than what is required to resolve or cope with the bad days or the problems.

On the other hand, Energy Drainers need no introduction or definition. You know them. I know them. We *all* know them. In fact, I can all but guarantee that the mere mention of the term Energy Drainer has just now caused at least one person to leap into the forefront of your mind. Being around Energy Drainers makes you feel as if someone has let all the air out of your tires. When you ask them how they are, they'll tell you—specifically, explicitly, and it's *never* good news. Are you familiar with the half full/half empty glass observation? An Energy Drainer's glass is not just half empty; the glass has a lipstick stain, an old cigarette butt in the bottom, and is full of dribble holes.

I will make this very easy on you: *Anyone* who tries to shut you down in any way when you attempt to discuss your loss is an Energy Drainer, someone who is more concerned with their feelings than they are with your healing. Let's put it another way. You have a beautiful 16x20 picture, for which you need a frame. Now, would you go out and buy a 3x5 frame for your 16x20 picture and reasonably expect it to fit? Of course not. So, why on Earth would you share a 16x20 picture of your devastating loss, your wounded heart, your roller-coaster emotions, and your healing journey in general . . . with someone who has a 3x5 mind?

Sharlene was facing what would have been her twenty-fifth wedding anniversary while also facing the three-year anniversary date of her husband's death. This left her feeling apprehensive—she knew that the day would be difficult. Shortly before the dreaded date, Sharlene was lunching with a friend (whom she once considered a member of her family) and brought up the fact that she was feeling a bit down; a feeling that most reasonable people would understand. She shares, "As we were waiting for our food to arrive, my friend said, 'You know what? He probably would have lived if you had loved him enough. He's gone and there's nothing you can do about it. It's time to flush the toilet and move on already.' I felt as though whatever was left of my heart just imploded. When my husband died, I constantly asked myself what more I could have done to keep him alive. I felt so guilty because I couldn't be with him more than I already had been, and my friend was well aware of this."

Aside from the horror of someone being told to metaphorically "flush the toilet" in reference to a person's life, legacies, and memories, as well as inferring that loving someone "enough" would have somehow magically rid them of whatever illness or infirmity took their life, this particular person actually transcends the concept of Energy Drainer. People like these are downright toxic to a healing journey. Fortunately, Sharlene was wise to quickly realize this fact. She also understood that this person had no business playing any part in her life, stating, "She was completely oblivious, spending the remainder of our time together whining about how horrible her husband was. Later that day, I posted what had happened on social media and announced that she was being eradicated from my life. Looking back, I now realize what an emotional vampire she was, feeding off the misery of others."

Taking Censorship One Step Further: Abandonment

Another issue that sadly walks hand-in-hand with grief censorship is that of the abandonment of the surviving spouse.[1] Susan

---

1 And, if applicable, their children as well.

says, "I've lost friends. You are a reminder of the worst possible nightmare that could happen to them, so they leave, and you are left standing amidst the rubble of your life." Sharlene adds, "The couples with whom we were once close have virtually disappeared. My husband was loved by so many people, and no doubt his death hit them hard. But once the funeral was over, everyone resumed their lives."

Loss attacks many aspects of your life, but perhaps somewhat surprisingly, none more than your address book. I experienced significant abandonment by former "friends" (coupled and otherwise) because they either wanted the return of Pre-Widow Carole (whom you met in Chapter Two, "Embracing the 'New' You"), or they simply did not know what to do, now that it was just myself and a young daughter. I was also precipitously abandoned by certain family members, leaving me alone to look into said daughter's confused, tear-filled eyes while desperately searching my mind for a reply to, "Mommy, I don't understand. Why don't they love me anymore?"

It's an unfortunate reality that some of the people who you once believed to be good friends—or even family—might choose to leave your life for a number of reasons. They may indeed be uncomfortable with being around you. Others may criticize your healing journey. Relationships may also fracture or self-destruct because of more tangible reasons (i.e., matters involving money, property, or other assets related to inheritance—or the lack thereof). Most disappointing and disgustingly all too common are those who believe that since becoming widowed, you have suddenly transformed into a scheming "man trap" or "babe magnet," ready to pounce on unsuspecting and innocent boyfriends, girlfriends, husbands, or wives in an imaginary attempt to spirit them away.

Choosing to Refuse and Refocus

I want you to think of your healing journey as a train. You are the engineer of the train and the people in your life are the passengers. As with any train, people get on board and people disembark at certain points. Some are on the train for a short time, some are on it for the long haul, and others never bother to board the train at all. As the engineer of your healing journey train, your job—your most important job—is to keep the train moving forward and on the track.

Especially after a profound loss, it's very easy to focus on who chooses to get off or stay off of your healing journey train, rather than keeping your focus where it belongs; on who is climbing aboard your train and on those who have chosen to *stay* on board throughout your loss experience *and* your journey. You can't properly engineer your train by constantly looking in a rearview mirror to see who has chosen to abandon both it and you. Focusing on those who choose to exit your life will bring you down and keep you there. It's negative energy focused on negative people who are not worthy of your focus, and who will never add to your healing in a positive way. Let them leave. They've made their choice.

Now, you make *your* choice: Choose to *refuse.* Refuse to live your life looking into a rearview mirror. Refuse to focus on who has willingly left your life for whatever reason. Focus instead on those climbing aboard, sitting down, strapping in, and staying on board with you for the ride that is your forward-moving healing journey . . . and beyond.

So how do you face both grief censorship and abandonment? Listen to those who have walked a similar path:

Susan: "Don't be afraid of the grief journey; learn to embrace it. It will not be easy. This will be most likely the hardest thing you will ever do, as your life has changed forever. But one day, you will be okay. You will have such a deep understanding of what life truly means and what living it means. I am okay, and you will be one day too. I promise."

Sharlene: "In many cases, people simply don't know what to say to you and will instead say anything just to feel less awkward. That doesn't mean you should remain silent. Speaking up is an opportunity to educate and inform the uninitiated about what it truly means to be bereaved."

Finally, if you are in a position of potential support to someone who is experiencing or has experienced bereavement, it may be very difficult for you, perhaps to the point of discomfort. No one is saying that you should not be upset or perhaps even moved to tears. By all means, be upset. Have feelings. Let the tears flow. These are all good things. However, remember that it's not about you at that particular moment; it's about the person who is seeking both comfort and hope.

Those in the bereaved community are quite cognizant of the fact that theirs is a sad and depressing situation, sometimes to the point of feeling self-conscious. Don't pile on to those feelings by shutting them down, or otherwise pronouncing that Grief Time is officially over, or that the imaginary statute of grief limitations has just run out with you. And *please* do not merely abandon them or choose to forget that they and their sadness both exist. I assure you that you will not catch a severe case of Death by discussing someone's loss or being a sympathetic ear and a loving source of support. Accept the discussion as the subliminal compliment that it is; out of everyone in the world, someone has chosen *you* with whom to share. It indicates trust in your heart and, should they be asking advice, your judgment.

Instead of a being a Sorrow Shut Down, choose instead to be a Safe Haven:

The kind ear. The gentle heart. The understanding soul.

The hand that offers hope.

EKITA!

When we hear the word *poverty*,

we tend to think only in terms of monetary poverty.

Being without.

Doing without.

. . . and a large amount of suffering.

❤

However, many widowed suffer from a different kind of poverty.

An emotional poverty, which also involves

being without.

Doing without

. . . and a large amount of suffering.

❤

Your life is not meant to be lived in *any* kind of poverty.

❤

You're not condemned to a life of emotional poverty

based upon or because of your loss experience.

❤

Some who surround you may say, think, or believe otherwise.

Let them.

❤

You don't have time for emotional-poverty thinking;
a headspace that will serve only to keep you
in a place of emotional poverty.
You have work to do.
You have healing to do.
You have a purpose to discover and fulfill.
You have a life to live.

♥

And if you're not quite "there" yet,
because your loss is new,
or because you feel stuck,
or because negative influence has stalled your healing . . .
that's okay.

♥

As long as you understand
that you are neither meant nor destined to live
a life bereft.
A life of emotional poverty.
Not now.
Not ever.

Bereavement
Boot Camp Lesson Four:
"I Turn to . . . *Who?*"

We are now at the Boot Camp halfway point, which is when people will usually do one of two things: give up out of frustration, or dig in with even more determination. Take a quick moment and look back over the last few Boot Camps. Have you completed (or at least attempted) any one or all of your Boot Camp challenges? Have you been reading (and re-reading) your affirmations and EKITAs? What are your results so far? How are you feeling? Do you feel like you've made any progress at all? Are you feeling even a *little* bit more enriched, empowered, and proactive? If you have done as much as use one affirmation, EKITA, or tried at least one challenge, congratulations —and keep going!

If you feel like you're having difficulty with any one or all of your challenges, that's okay. Sometimes kicking grief in the ass takes a little more time. Take as much time with your personal ass-kicking as you need; there are no deadlines. Hold on to your challenges and give them another try in a week or two. Continue to use your affirmations and EKITAs every single day as positive reinforcement that you *are* taking steps forward on your healing journey, no matter how small you think those steps may be. Now is *not* the time to quit.

Speaking of positivity, I'll warn you that this Boot Camp lesson may be a bit tough for you. Actually, it may be a *lot* tougher for you. In this lesson, I'm calling on you to take what you've just learned from the last chapter and actually use it to jettison negativity. This is a challenging assignment that I hope you will not only accept, but embrace as well.

Critics, Critics Everywhere

Look around you—they are everywhere.

Critics.

Nowadays, there are critics in virtually every area of our lives: from movies, music, art, and the theater, to food, clothing trends, and (Lord, help me) books. The advent of the Internet has only served to expand both the ability and desire to criticize (whether deserved or not) and, in many cases, with the added advantage of complete anonymity. Rather than only those critics who weigh in on the movies we see, the concerts we attend, and the clothes we wear, the facility to criticize has since extended to the "Everyday Joe/Jane," who can now write a lengthy review on any number of websites if exception is taken to a newspaper article, an overcooked cheeseburger, or an unpleasant hotel stay.

Unfortunately for millions of widowed, critics have invaded their lives as well. Perhaps you too have personally experienced the insensitive post-loss judgment of critics, striking at a time when you have never felt more vulnerable or ill-equipped to handle it. Some of your critics might be relatives, others may be so-called friends or acquaintances, and still others might be those with whom you work. These self-styled experts on the subject of "Your Life and How to Live It" may be imparting criticism on everything from the floral arrangements at the funeral to the food served afterward, from how you're handling yourself emotionally, to whether or not you choose to keep or sell your beloved's collection of vintage hood ornaments.

Aside from the obvious lack of compassion so badly needed during a difficult time, the primary problem is that the people whom critics target are actually paying attention to what is being said. Moreover, not only do these poor people lend far too much credence to criticism, they begin to question their own instincts and best judgment as to their healing processes.

Be they past or present, whoever the critics may be in your life, this I know to be true: They are not *you*. No one—not *one* person— who ventures criticism or observation as to how you're handling your none-too-easy healing journey is *you*, and therefore immediately loses the right to criticize. What if the exceptional occurs and one or more of the critics in your life has suffered a loss experience that is similar to the loss that you've endured? They *still* are not you and, for that reason, they are *still* not entitled to criticize.

The Uniqueness and Strength That Is You

If every single one of us is unique as a person, it then naturally follows that every single healing journey is unique as well. Never *ever* should another person's journey (or anything in connection with a healing journey) be criticized. It's fine to gently advise or make suggestions, but only when asked to do so and never in a disparaging manner. Whether "constructively" or otherwise,[1] no one has the right to criticize how anyone suffering a loss handles *anything*—from whether or not they visit a gravesite (be it sooner, later, or ever) to a decision to sell everything that they own and sail around the world.

One of the things that the loss experience also offers to us is an opportunity to examine where we have been, what we have been through, where we are today, and where we want to go from this point forward. While you are making that examination and while you are figuring out how to deal with any self-appointed critics who may have invaded your life, I would encourage you to grab and hold on to one word:

Strength

Since your loss, you have likely already heard over and over about how "strong" you are, or how strong you have to be for your children, or how your loved one wanted you to be strong. I also understand that "strong" may be either the last thing that you are feeling right now, or the last thing that you *want* to feel right now.

---

1 There is no such thing as "constructive criticism." It's a most ridiculous phrase and one of the biggest oxymorons on the planet—ranking right up there with "jumbo shrimp," "mild turbulence," and "quick shopping trip."

However, the strength that I'm talking about is not the paste-on-a-smile, put-on-an-act-for-the-world strength that at one time or another we all feel compelled to portray. The kind of strength that I'm talking about comes from within you; the little voice that you must now turn into a great big voice. Find your inner voice. Locate that strength center. Use that strength center to face the critics and let them know in no uncertain terms that you are doing the very best that you can—in *your* way and in *your* own time.

Remember, too, that critics will eventually find someone or something else to criticize. You will soon become old news. Critics generally have too much time on their hands, and instead of being active and positive contributors to your life specifically and to humanity in general, they instead wish to tear others down or apart. Let them carry on. You have other far more important things to do. You have healing to accomplish. You have people to meet who will nurture and care about you. You have a life to live.

No More Negativity

The fact is sad but true: we're constantly surrounded by negativity. Don't believe me? All you need to do is turn on the television —and I'm not even talking about the evening news. In recent years it seems as though most television programming promotes, encourages, and reinforces negativity, be it through despicable behavior, deplorable schemes designed to humiliate, deliberately setting out to hurt others by word or deed, or indulging in general pot-stirring when the pot is empty . . . all ostensibly in the name of entertainment. In fact, when one reality star[2] was recently questioned about the

---

2 I am using the terms "reality" and "star" begrudgingly and very loosely.

behavior that takes place regularly on her show, she nonchalantly shrugged, laughed, and replied, "It's entertaining." You read that correctly. Apparently people's pain equals entertainment. Seriously?

It is therefore hardly a surprise that given the current cultural environment, combined with society's overall reluctance to deal with or even discuss loss, you may be met with less-than-enthusiastic support on your healing journey. For example, has anyone ever made any one (or more) of the following statements to you? [3]

- ✓ "You should be over it already."
- ✓ "You can't possibly . . . (date again, remain on your own, sell your house, keep your house, or otherwise decide to do something that you wish to do)."
- ✓ "You should have closure by now."
- ✓ "You think *you* have it bad?" (This statement will be immediately followed by a tale of woe that someone will find comparable to your widowhood. Whether or not it actually is comparable will likely be up for debate.)
- ✓ "It's been long enough. You need to snap out of it."
- ✓ "Aren't you afraid of what people will say (or think) if you . . . (fill in the blank with something else that you want to do that is being met with disapproval or judgment)?"

If you've ever been the recipient of these or similar statements or attitudes, it's my job as both author and Boot Camp Master to remind you that *you are talking to the wrong people!*

Now, I'm the first to acknowledge that you can't completely eliminate any and all negativity in your life, any more than you

---

3 Or comparable sentiments that would take far too long to list.

can eliminate any and all stress. It's impossible. But why would you deliberately choose to share the trials and triumphs, the valleys and peaks, and the twists-and-turns of your healing journey with someone who can't be bothered to even attempt to be supportive? I've just finished waxing poetic about Energy Drainers (which obviously includes self-appointed critics), but I also realize that everyone has these people in their lives, myself included. You might work with them, they might be a part of your social circle, you might even be related to them. However, while Energy Drainers may indeed be a part of your life, they don't need to be integrally *involved* in your life, especially where your healing journey is concerned. These are *not* people who are truly interested in your life, let alone your loss or your challenges. These are *not* people who are going to support you. These are *not* people who are going to lift you up, encourage you, or otherwise provide you with anything other than negativity.

Stop sharing with these people! Just *stop* it. Right *now.*

Remember that, widowed or not, when anyone says that you "can't" or "shouldn't" do something, they're essentially putting *their* life decisions onto you. Think of one Energy Drainer in your life right now who is quick to negative opinion, judgment, or use of the words, "can't" or "shouldn't." Now ask yourself:

Why am I sharing with them?

Why am I listening to them?

Why am I lending importance, significance, or any gravitas to what they are saying?

If you can't come up with solid reasons or positive responses to these questions, you have just answered these questions for yourself.

To be clear, the Energy Drainers in your life don't necessarily want to hurt you, but they don't necessarily want to help you, either. They are *not* positive, they are *not* going to be encouraging, and they are not going to be supportive. They will instead say things like, "Support groups don't work," or "What help do you expect to find in a book?" or, "Bereavement Boot Camp? That sounds stupid."[4]

The reality is that Energy Drainers don't want you to be happy because *they* have chosen to be unhappy. Energy Drainers do not want you to succeed because *they* have chosen to be unsuccessful. They want *you* to decide the same way that *they* have decided, and *their* decision is to remain miserable. *They* are trying to design your destiny and if you let them, they will succeed. You simply cannot allow that to happen. Remember what you just learned in the last chapter: you can't share a 16x20 vision of your healing journey and your life's design with someone who has a 3x5 mind.

Your time wasted traveling down Negativity Highway with the citizens of Bittertown and Angryville has come to an end. It's *finished*. It's *over*. You are *done*. The nature of loss in and of itself is a negative experience, and while there is nothing that we can do about the experience itself, we *are* in control of our reactions to the experience. This includes the people whom we invite into—or dismiss from—our lives.

Understand that just as with finding your strength, eliminating negativity does not mean that you stick a make-believe smile on your face and walk around every single day singing, "Walking on Sunshine" whether you feel like it or not. Eliminating negativity simply requires you to make every effort to surround yourself with

---

4 Again, these are actual quotes folks.

people who understand what it is that you've been through, that from which you are recovering, and who are willing to stand by you with ready shoulders (on which to lean), open hearts (used in listening honestly and lovingly), and open arms (to give the hug for which every single one of us yearns). These are not "yes" people, for those who love you will also be honest with you if they feel that you might be coping in a manner that could be detrimental to your health and welfare. However, they'll approach you in a warm, loving, respectful, and *nonjudgmental* manner.

You don't have time, energy, or necessity for anyone who is any less than a strong source of support in your life. If those "less-than" people *do* exist in your life, they are no longer part of your healing journey. *Period.* Energy Drainers may be a part of your life out of necessity or obligation, but that *doesn't mean* that they are entitled to be an intimate part of one of the most important journeys you'll ever experience: your healing journey.

Here's your fourth, halfway-point Boot Camp Affirmation. Keep it in front of you.

I will limit time spent with critics and Energy Drainers and will instead seek and welcome those who contribute to my life in positive ways. On my difficult days or during those difficult periods of time when I feel that the faith I have in myself or in my healing journey is wavering, I will turn only to those who will breathe belief into me, rather than turn to those who might bring me down or are already bringing me down.

Boot Camp Challenge

Make two lists. You'll write the first list on the next page, comprised of at least five Energy Givers to whom you already are turning or to whom you will turn for positive support, input, encouragement, and reinforcement. Note their names, along with a brief reason as to why they are part of your Energy Giver circle. Afterward, tell them about your participation in Bereavement Boot Camp, why you have selected them as one of your five (because if nothing else, we sometimes forget to say thank you to the people who get us through the "getting through"), and make yourself accountable to them. Share your challenges, ask for suggestions, and commit to truly integrating their positivity into your healing journey.

Now, get a separate sheet of blank paper. Be brutally honest with yourself as you make a second list of five people whom you consider to be the most prominent Energy Drainers in your life. List their names, *why* you consider them to be Energy Drainers (so you are acutely aware of exactly why they're on your list), and then re-read the above affirmation as you *tear up* that list. Keep the torn-up pieces in a small bowl on your bathroom or kitchen counter, or in a box next to your bed—anywhere that you'll regularly see that shredded list. Those torn-up pieces rep-

resent exactly what Energy Drainers are capable of doing to you and will serve as a reminder that they are *no longer permitted* to be an integral part of your healing journey. Remember, pay close attention to the EKITA! immediately following this lesson . . . and journey *forward*.

My Five Energy Givers

Name: Their energy-giving gift in my life is:

1. _____
2. _____
3. _____
4. _____
5. _____

Any more to add?

6. _____
7. _____
8. _____
9. _____
10. _____

My Energy Drainers

1. _____
2. _____
3. _____
4. _____
5. _____

While creating and shredding my list of Energy Drainers, I feel:

_____

_____

_____

EKITA!

It's a fact that we become like the five people with
whom we spend the most time.
Take a good look at your five.
Take a really good, long, hard, honest look.
Who are they?

❤

Make absolutely sure that you're choosing to
spend most of your very valuable time
with Energy Givers who support your journey in
positive and uplifting ways,
rather than spending too much time with negative people
who will steal your energy,
bring you down,
waste your time,
and discourage you from leading the life that you wish to design
and so richly deserve.

Say *What?* What Never to Say to the Widowed (and What to Say Instead)

" **I** don't know what to say."

"I'm afraid of saying the wrong thing."

The number of times I've heard these sentiments expressed by those who surround the widowed are countless. Unfortunately, many seem to have lost sight of the fact that the words, "I am so sorry" can be the most comforting words of all. As a result, and even though it may be in an attempt to console, people can instead wind up saying some pretty ridiculous things. Having been at the receiving end of some of these comments (and worse), I continue to be amazed at what some say in the guise of sympathy.

Following are actual expressions of "compassion" that have been shared, followed by what oftentimes goes through widowed's minds when hearing them. We will call this, "What *Not* to Say . . . Ever":

When someone says, "At least you were prepared." (When death is anticipated.)

What the widowed are thinking is, *Expecting death doesn't make reality any easier.*

When someone says, "At least s/he didn't suffer." (When death is sudden.)

What the widowed are thinking is, *That made things easier on them, not me.*

When someone says, "Everything happens for a reason."

What the widowed are thinking is, *Whatever that reason is, I'm not interested in hearing it.*

When someone says, "You were just meant to be alone."

What the widowed are thinking is, *If I were meant to be alone, I wouldn't have gotten married in the first place.*

When someone says, "I know how you feel."

What the widowed are thinking is, *No you don't, because you are not me.*

When someone says, "You'll find someone else."

What the widowed are thinking is, *What gave you the idea that I'm looking for someone else right now?*

When someone says, "Now you'll have closure."

What the widowed are thinking is, *What does that even mean? I don't want to "close" any part of my life.*

When someone says, "S/He's in a better place."

What the widowed are thinking is, *Better than here with me?*

When someone says, "You can always get a pet to replace him/her."

What the widowed are thinking is, *You're kidding, right?*

When someone says, "Divorce is the same."

What the widowed are thinking is, *It's not the same. I understand that you have experienced the death of a relationship. But with divorce, someone somewhere made a choice. No one chose to leave my marriage.*[1]

When someone says, "You were married for so many years and he/she lived a long life."

What the widowed are thinking is, *That doesn't matter. It will never be long enough.*

When someone says, "You're not really a widow/er because you were only married for a short time."

What the widowed are thinking is, *I missed the part of the wedding ceremony that said how long we had to be married before it "counted" toward widowhood.*

When someone says, "You weren't married, so you're not really widowed."

What the widowed are thinking is, *My heart doesn't understand technicalities. My heart only knows that the person with whom I planned to spend the rest of my life is gone.*

When someone says, "S/He was my brother/sister/other relative. You weren't really related."

What the widowed are thinking is, *Please make sure that I'm standing there when you tell our children that Mom and Dad weren't really related.*

---

1 See Chapter Eighteen ("The Epic Struggle: Death Versus Divorce").

The common thread in all of these statements (and many more like them) is that while most may be said in an attempt to comfort, absolutely none of these statements will console anyone. To the contrary, these statements can be extremely hurtful.

Here are a few more do's and don'ts of what to say to someone who is widowed.

Don'ts

Don't make remarks about how they don't look like a widow/er. Widowhood has many complexions; there is no "typical."

Don't remind a widowed how much time they had with their beloved prior to death or remark how "lucky" they are. First, the widowed are acutely aware of how long they were with their spouse; they need no reminders. More importantly, and as you learned in Chapter Six ("How Long Were You Married"), whether they were together for many decades or a few minutes, that time together was not long enough. Absolutely *no one* who has lost their spouse is feeling "lucky." Not. At. All.

Conversely, don't tell a widowed who was not married for very long (or was not married at all) that their spouse's/partner's death should not be a painful experience for them, or that "getting over it" should be easier. If love is love, it naturally follows that loss is loss. A love tragically lost should be honored, respected, and appropriate comfort offered, as love also does not recognize timetables or the presence of certificates (or lack thereof).

Don't begin any sentence with the words, "At least . . . ". The very word *least* automatically trivializes and diminishes both their organic feelings and whatever it is they are trying to convey. "At least" is reductive in tone, intent, and in nature. Whether or not you agree with their feelings is inconsequential. You can't tell someone how they feel and, at that moment, it's not about you. It is about someone who is trying to tell you something. Listen. Sympathize. Care.

Do's

Do express genuine sympathy: "I'm so sorry; I can't even begin to imagine the pain you're in right now." You've just provided immediate comfort and a sense of reassurance to someone whose world has been rocked, as well as reassurance that they don't have to face this bleakest of seasons on their own.

Do encourage dialogue: One of the most helpful things in the world is a kind ear. It will be after the funeral (when everyone else has seemingly disappeared) that your compassion is needed the most. Encourage—or better yet, initiate—a healthy and open dialogue with, "You might not be ready to talk about it today, but when you're ready, I'm here and I am ready to listen."

You really can be the first avenue of comfort to a widowed. No longer are the excuses, "I don't know what to say" or, "I'm afraid of saying the wrong thing" acceptable. While I'm not sure that I ever bought into the cliché that "Ignorance is bliss," this I know for certain: When it comes to consoling the bereaved, ignorance is *not* bliss. It is instead a gigantic *miss*.

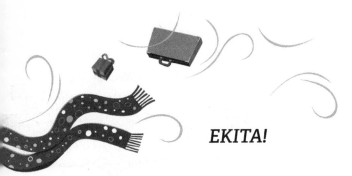

EKITA!

Death ends only a physical presence on earth.
It doesn't end love. It doesn't end memories.
It doesn't end the impact that those whom we dearly love had
and will continue to have on our lives.

❤

Death doesn't end anything other than
a person's physical journey alongside of us.

❤

And while it's incredibly painful to be left behind
by those whom we love,
We also have it within our power to carry on all of the legacies
that have been entrusted to our loving care.

❤

We have it in our power to choose how those sacred legacies will be
fulfilled by laughing, by loving, by exploring, by trying, by daring,
by giving, by sharing, by chasing, by dreaming, by doing, by *living*.
Think about the legacies that have been left to you by those you love
who have journeyed beyond their earthly bond.
Use the incredible power of those legacies.
Choose to both live and proudly carry forward those legacies.
Every single day.

CHAPTER
14

The Inalienable Right
to Grieve

L et me ask you what may sound like a stupid question.

Who is entitled to grieve the loss of their spouse?

I told you it would sound like a stupid question, and, by all measure, it should be considered as such. Our immediate and collective response to this question should be: "Anyone who is feeling overwhelming grief, loss, sadness, anger, fear (and so much more) after spousal loss is clearly *entitled* to grieve and should grieve accordingly. After all, the grieving process itself is the pathway to healing. Why on earth should anyone be denied this basic human right?"

Society's actual response to what is indeed a stupid question just might surprise you.

The widow was dressed traditionally and impeccably. She sat in a beautiful church, witnessing a touching funeral service and trying desperately to be the same pillar of strength for and comfort to her children that all widowed parents try to be during one of the worst experiences of their lives. Despite her valiant attempts, the look on her face was a twisted and pained mask of devastating grief. She had loved only one man in her entire life and spent most of her life with him. She had put her stratospheric career on hold more than once in order to care for him throughout the occurrence and subsequent recurrence of his illness. Now he was gone.

Undoubtedly, the very same questions swirled through her mind as they did (and do) in the minds of those of us who have sat in that very same place:

Who am I now?
What do I do now?
How do I face tomorrow?
How do I help my children when I don't even know how to help myself?

Yet when her loss was made public, much of the commentary was outright vitriolic. Why? The widow was Celine Dion, a woman who is beautiful, talented, and wealthy beyond most people's imagination or reach. Further, because she is Celine Dion, who will not know the financial trials with which many widowed are forced to cope (including yours truly), the tragically cruel and largely anonymous consensus was that she apparently had no business mourning her lost husband.

☙

"What is she crying for? She has her millions to console her."

"Excuse me, but why should we feel sorry for her?"

"It's not like she has a reason to be sad. If she had money problems like normal people, then she'd have a reason to be sad."

Every time I think that I have honestly seen it all, I'm proven
wrong.

These are just a small sampling of the comments received in
response to an interview that I gave with regard to Celine Dion's
return to the stage after the loss of her husband René Angélil to a
long battle with cancer. Rather than garnering any real sympathy
or compassion, there were sadly dozens more comments similar to
these (including some that are unprintable) that littered the bottom pages of the article which had been published internationally
across numerous media outlets.

As I skimmed through the toxic opinions, I was stunned. Does
wealth or the lack of money concerns due to inheritance, pre-
planning measures, or simply being rich in one's own right mean
that one is no longer a human being with human feelings? Does
wealth eliminate one's inherent right to grieve the loss of a spouse?

The answer is *no*.

Rolling around in wads of cash[1] or marveling over one's plen-
tiful bank accounts does not eradicate loss, bereavement, and the
very real need to grieve.

Does the presence of abundant finances lessen the weight
of financial woes? Obviously. Along with a great majority of my
widowed brothers and sisters, I, too, was left sitting in a financial

---

[1] Judging by some of the comments, this is what people were apparently imagining Ms. Dion to be doing.

quagmire from which it took years of hard work to extricate. I well remember the days of having to choose between making a full mortgage payment or making the payment on Kendall's braces. Financial burden post-widowhood indeed becomes the root of many anxious days and many sleepless nights.

However, I don't believe that the mere presence of money would, should, or does erase grief; nor does it erase the need—and the right—to grieve. While financial woes might not necessarily top the list of one who is widowed and wealthy or who is left "comfortably,"[2] the financially well-off widowed most certainly have the same worries, doubts, fears, anger, have-to's, and grief as do the rest of us.

I also rapidly discovered that wealth was not the only supposed preclusion to the right to grieve. Apparently, if a death is anticipated (as was my situation with Mike and as it is with anyone dealing with a terminal illness or long-term infirmity), you should already be "prepared" for the inevitability of death, thus removing the right to mourn.

The list continues. If you are married for many years, you are considered "lucky" and should be feeling only gratitude, rather than grief (see Chapter Six, "How Long Were You Married?"). It also seems that if one experiences multiple losses in relatively close proximity to one another, accusations of being a "drama queen" or "sympathy junkie" will furiously fly. Then of course there is the all-too-familiar game of one-upmanship, also known as "My Pain Is Worse than Your Pain." In this game with no winners, others try to compare their losses (or other woes) as being worse than the

---

2 More bluntly and insensitively referred to as having "widowed well."

person experiencing loss in the immediate. I mean, why in the name of common sense would *anyone* look at another and say, "You were only married for X years and I was married for Y years, so my loss is so much more difficult"?

It is a refrain that I am compelled to make far too often for my liking and will repeat here once again: If love is love, it naturally follows that loss is loss. Period. Loss doesn't need qualification, justification, or vindication—and neither does the accompanying grief, mourning, and bereavement when loss invades and (for a time) commandeers your life. Wealth, anticipatory death, multiple losses in close proximity, or anything inadvertently left off of this list doesn't deny anyone the right to grieve, mourn, and embark upon their healing journey. Additionally, the last time I checked, there was no statute of limitations as to the number of times one is entitled to go through the grieving process. As you will later learn in Chapter Seventeen ("Does One Grief Fit All?"), you are entitled to grieve each loss experience as the individual losses that they are. You are not limited in your mourning in any way, and you should rail against anyone who attempts to impose those limits— for *any* reason.

As you learned in an earlier EKITA, grief is the painfully difficult price that we pay for loving with all of our hearts and everything that we are. Loss is, in fact, an unavoidable part of a life that includes loving others. Loving others also guarantees one more thing: our inalienable right to grieve. And just as with any other rights to which we are entitled as human beings, let no one deny you this very basic right . . . for *any* reason.

EKITA!

What did your loss take away from you?

It took your spouse.

But he or she was not all that was taken from you.

❤

You were also robbed of a life being lived,

of goals being set,

of dreams being realized,

and a future being planned.

❤

Children were robbed of a parent

and the joy of growing into adulthood

with their now-absent parent watching proudly and cheering loudly.

This is a tremendous amount for one set of tragic circumstances to

take away.

❤

So why would you then permit the circumstances

that stole your spouse

to take anything more from you?

❤

If you're not pursuing your healing journey

in the ways that you wish,
this is exactly what you are allowing death to do.

❤

You can't help the circumstances surrounding
your beloved's death,
but what you do from this point forward can be designed.
You have that control.

❤

You can choose how to react to people who are
less than supportive or positive.
You can choose the avenues of support that best speak to you
(because those avenues are different for everyone)
and make use of each and every single one.
You can choose to do one positive thing every day
that will move you in the healing direction in which you wish to go.

❤

Have you taken the control?
All you have to do is choose it.
Right now.

❤

Refuse to give your loss circumstances any more
than those circumstances have already taken from you.
Whatever they may be,
Those circumstances have already taken enough.

CHAPTER
15

Enough Hurt—
Where Is the Hope?

I must have had a very confused look on my face when it happened.

It was the same look I've seen on our cat when she saw a talking parrot in the waiting room of the veterinarian's office. It's the same look that I get on my face when I hear about the multi-millions of dollars that multi-millions of women spend to have their breasts enlarged . . . and then I read articles in various women's magazines that teach how to minimize a large bust line. Utter and complete confusion.

I had observed numerous complaints from widowed who were leaving various support organizations and online support groups (including our own) because of the "negative and depressing" (direct quote) posts being shared by widowed. I received many e-mails, complaint after complaint, that essentially stated, "I'm here looking for hope. All I see is people talking about how awful life is and how awful it's always going to be. I can't take this."

Obviously concerned about anyone feeling as though life was always going to be an exercise in pain, grief, and raw mourning, and thereafter leaving these various communities of hope and support to try to cope alone, I perhaps unwisely chose to share these sentiments within the widowed community. Instead of being met with compassion and understanding for the widowed who with these concerns, I was instead the recipient of very defensive and hurtful responses.

So there I was, just like my cat in the veterinarian's office. *Baffled.*

How could people who were all in the very same boat not understand how others might feel at constantly reading discouraging posts, knowing full well how emotions can crest and cave, wax and wane—sometimes from hour to hour. It didn't sound right; it certainly didn't feel right. I second-guessed my judgment on broaching the subject to other widowed and thought that perhaps I should have remained silent on this apparently growing issue.

Which is more important: conveying hope for the future? Or sharing hurt in the present?

Then I had an, *"Oh yeah, now I remember what I'm doing here"* moment. I remembered that we are here to serve everyone in the widowed community. *Everyone.* Even if there is disagreement or dissension, the people who were and are leaving support organizations and social media forums in droves because they feel that the atmosphere is overwhelmingly negative and hopeless still deserve to be heard; as do the people who so badly need these very same places to vent their true, organic, authentic feelings.

Those who are feeling truly, organically, and authentically grief-stricken, sad, angry, overwhelmed, depressed, abandoned, confused, frightened and/or completely lost should be able to voice their feelings honestly, even though their feelings may be negative or discouraging to read. They have a right to be heard and need to be able to exercise that right in safe places among others who understand the widowhood journey. After all, most of us either have been or are now surrounded by people who simply do not grasp the widowhood experience. Must the widowed now be afraid of honestly expressing themselves within their own community as well?

Yup. It's pretty confusing. However (and this is important), no matter where you fall on the spectrum, *you deserve to be heard. You* deserve to be helped. *You* deserve to receive what you need in the way of support, whenever you need it. Can hurt and hope coexist? Yes it can. However, it takes understanding on both sides of the issue.

To those of you who are either contemplating leaving or who have left online pages, support forums, support organizations, or any support groups (online or in person) because of "negative and depressing" remarks and writings, remember that these places exist for the common purpose of giving the widowed community a sense of *community*. This means that anyone within the community must and should be able to freely express how they are feeling at any given moment, how they are coping, and, most importantly, feel comfortable in asking for help. Whichever forum they choose, whatever the mode of expression, it is perhaps the one place that they can go and be who they are in the moment, without fear of judgment or recrimination.

Most importantly, don't unilaterally decide that just because someone else is sad, depressed, or scared, that your journey is going to be identical. The fact is that your healing journey can be however *you* fashion it. The bottom line is that you will gravitate toward that which you focus on. If you are in need of positivity and hope, focus and connect with the positivity and hope in these support groups and organizations rather than choosing to focus on only the negative aspects, falsely concluding that absolutely everyone is "negative and depressing" and choosing instead to cope alone.

To those who were or are less tolerant upon hearing these complaints, or who have no patience for the widowed who are, in fact, searching for a beacon of hope in a seemingly endless sea of darkness, you too are called upon to show understanding. We are talking about other widowed. We're talking about people who want to be positive and proactive in their healing, and positivity and pro-activity should always be encouraged. These are people who are making a courageous choice to heal and move forward. These are people who desperately want to hear that there is life after loss, triumph after tragedy, and hope after hurt. They want to be told, "I was where you are and I'm getting through it, one day at a time." They want to learn how to do the same. Constantly seeing or hearing story after story that seem to indicate otherwise can indeed be discouraging. You absolutely have every right to vent and express yourself, but you also need to be compassionate and show grace toward those who need to see other kinds of messages as well: Messages of hope. Messages of promise. Messages of healing. Messages that convey, "I may be down, but I don't have to stay down. I'm going to get better and I'm going to use every single avenue that will help get me to a place of peace."

The lesson is clear. By acknowledging that hurt and hope are part of the healing journey and that we must welcome and embrace every person at every stage of that journey, both hurt and hope can coexist. Let's embrace that concept—and move forward together.

EKITA!

So many widowed feel like they "had it all"
and then "had it all taken away," and you're certainly not wrong.
However, if you had it all once,
you can have it all again.

❤

Having it all doesn't require the presence of another person.
It doesn't require that you remain in the same place
and do the same things
if that's not what is in your heart to do.

❤

You are not the same person post-widowhood
and, because you are not the same person,
"having it all" may mean something entirely different now
than what it once meant to you.

❤

"All" doesn't come quickly.
"All" will not look exactly as it once did.
The new "all" is likely not what you expected it to be.

❤

Getting and staying proactive with your healing
is your key to having it all once again.
Whatever it looks like today,
your "all" is out there
and it's waiting for you.

❤

Don't let the pain of the past
determine your possibilities and your tomorrows.
Remind yourself every single day
that you indeed deserve to have a brand-new "all."

Bereavement Boot Camp
Lesson Five:
Put Your Tits on Your Back

W elcome to Bereavement Boot Camp Lesson Five. You have probably noticed that as you progress through the book, the subject matter, the talk, and the challenges all get a little tougher—but then again, so have you. If you've been utilizing the affirmations, reviewing the EKITAs, and at least attempting the challenges, you may very well be feeling a bit stronger and a lot more empowered . . . which is great, because you're about to put that strength and empowerment to good use right now.

In follow up to learning about Energy Givers and Energy Drainers, you will now learn how to quit conducting your healing journey and your life in general according to the opinions of those who surround you.

Right now, you're thinking about one of two things: you are either sitting there thinking, *Yeah right, Carole. Easier said than done,* or you're thinking about skipping this chapter altogether because you believe this to be an impossible task. I hope that you choose not to skip over the chapter and, if you're thinking *Easier said than done,* you would be incorrect. It is neither easy to say, nor is it easy to do.[1]

So how do we approach this very challenging lesson? By putting our tits on our backs. Stay with me—it will all make sense in a few minutes.

I. Love. Cher. Yes, *that* Cher. There—I said it.

My fan-girl obsession with Cher began at the ripe old age of mid-single digits with the releases of "I Got You Babe" and "The Beat Goes On," and thereafter went into full overdrive with the premiere of *The Sonny & Cher Comedy Hour,* a television show that launched a thousand "I'm gonna be *that* when I grow up" fantasies. I even wrote a fan letter and received a response—a letter I still have to this day.[2]

Cher. The clothes; the costumes; the quips; the waist-length, sleek and shiny mane of jet-black hair; the should-be-trademarked, disdainful mane-of-hair flip . . . in my oh-very-young starry eyes, she was a goddess. But perhaps even more than all of the Cher icing that was the object of my pre-adolescent envy was her *attitude.* She always remained true to herself, regardless of what anyone said or thought. She did her Cher thing in her Cher way,

---

1 I know this to be true, because I, too, have had to say and do both.

2 Okay, it was a "form" letter, the exact same letter that I am confident millions of other kids received as well—but still . . .

and she never bothered to poll the delegations for opinions or for approval. She had her head on straight, she listened intently to her heart, she always stood up for what she believed to be good and right, and she never shied away from anyone dumb enough to take her on. In her own words: "I've always taken risks, and never worried what the world might really think of me."

As with most any other subject, Cher was extremely candid and forthcoming about the fact that she chose to undergo cosmetic surgery. An unfair, yet apparently growing necessity in the world of entertainment and public forum, she obviously also felt quite comfortable with her decision. However, her frankness and honesty did not keep the critics at bay; most of them were buoyed years later by the integration of social media into the conversation. It seemed as though anyone and everyone felt some kind of simultaneous moral superiority and self-imposed right to unkindly hazard opinion upon her surgical decision making.

Finally becoming fed up with the public discourse, Cher took control of the conversation and reminded the world at large that both her body and her life belonged to her, famously stating: "If I want to put my tits on my back, it's nobody's business but my own."

I figured that since this attitude and overall outlook has worked quite well for Cher throughout the decades, it could work for me— and it can work for you as well. So with apologies to the gentlemen readers, when it comes to our healing journey, let's start eschewing any negative, unsupportive opinions . . . and put our tits on our backs.

Confession time 2.0: By both nature and DNA hardwiring, I am the perennial cheerleader—the "anti-Cher," if you will. I was always the person who gallantly tried to make everyone happy and garner the approval of everyone in my orbit; a phenomenon now referred to as "people pleasing." I also own the reality that I occasionally (and to my detriment) actually permitted the opinions of those who simply don't matter to get the better of me, at least momentarily. Once I finally discovered how to put my tits on my back where my own healing journey (and the rest of my life) was concerned, the lessons came quickly and life became much easier. I hope that I can expedite those lessons for you and ease your life path as well.

During Bereavement Boot Camp Lesson Two, you discovered that your healing journey actually belongs to *you*. While this is a great discovery and a huge step forward in and of itself, you must now start *believing* it. True belief consists of more than simply turning a deaf ear to the "Aren't you over it" and "Why are you/ aren't you . . ." comments that most of us have heard and that you may be coping with even now. True belief means that it's now time to start choosing to do whatever it is that *you* want to do to begin healing, further your healing journey, or move on to the next phase of your journey—*without* first polling the world at large. These things might include, but certainly are not limited to:

- ✓ Making a decision about your ring(s), whether that decision is to keep wearing it/them, move it/them to your right hand, take it/them off altogether, or having it/them repurposed into a new piece of jewelry.
- ✓ Taking a vacation, even if that vacation is during the holidays, an "angelversary," or any other time when people might be likely to disapprove of or otherwise question your choice.
- ✓ Going through and/or making decisions concerning your beloved's belongings.

✓ Either moving out of or choosing to remain in your home.

✓ Returning to work, changing jobs or careers, or retiring altogether.

✓ Pursuing a new hobby or interest, or picking up where you left off with a current hobby or interest.

✓ Deciding whether dating again is right for you at this point or at any point on your journey, and then pursuing the avenue that you choose.

While there are obviously many more, I enumerate these moments because they are (a) the moments about which I've received the most mail, and (b) the moments that are most often subject to opinion, solicited or otherwise.

In Bereavement Boot Camp Lesson Four, you were challenged to jettison the Energy Drainers and critics from your life and, if unable to eliminate them from your life altogether, you were challenged to prevent them from being intimately involved with your healing journey. Hopefully, you now understand why. Energy Drainers may very likely be the same people from whom you are either seeking opinions (which is counterintuitive, to say the least), or they are venturing their own negative and unsupportive opinions without being asked, opinions that you may very well permit to keep you from moving forward.

When you ask someone what they think if you (fill in the blank with something that is really in your heart to do—or not to do), what you are *actually* saying is, "I really want to/don't want to do this thing and I really need you to support me in that decision/choice/goal." Unfortunately, Energy Drainers are not going to give you the support that you seek, and you will ultimately wind up feeling worse for having shared with the wrong person (or people).

Here's the rub. When you seek opinions from Energy Drainers (consciously or otherwise), you are likely going to use *their* opinions to formulate *your* decision making in the moment and/or your overall opinion of you as a person. For example, let's say that you and Energy Drainer are having a cocktail. You wrangle your courage and get up the nerve to share, "I'm thinking of dating again. What do you think?" Energy Drainer is perhaps a little jealous or thinks that you should be wearing the proverbial black veil forever, and the response is something akin to, "How could you do that?" or "Don't you love him/her anymore?" or "That is so inappropriate," or some other similar nonsense.

After hearing these (or comparable) responses, I promise that without fail, your immediate thought processes will be negative. You're now thinking, *Of course I still love him/her* or *Maybe it is inappropriate* or, *What's wrong with me?* or, *How could I even think about dating again?* or some other similar nonsense (intentionally repeated).

Your conclusive thought will then be: *It's official. I'm a terrible person.* Voilà. Not only has someone just wrested away your control, you now have an extra helping of lousy self-opinion to go along with it, an opinion that was just dictated by *someone else*. You thereafter mentally skulk away from the conversation with Energy Drainer, feeling terrible about your future and, even worse, feeling absolutely terrible about yourself.

I know firsthand how hard it is to find the determination and the strength to do whatever it is you have in your heart to do, despite the opinions of those around you. I also know that staying true to yourself and your healing journey can compromise or even cost relationships. However, the very important bottom line is that at the end of the day, *you* are the only person living your life. *You* are the one who has to live with the decisions that you make, not the person venturing opinions and eventually casting judgment upon decisions and choices that have nothing to do with them or their life.

To be blunt (because this *is* Boot Camp), judgments are reserved for actual judges and the courtrooms over which they preside. If you are of a spiritual nature, judgment is also reserved for your higher power. That's about it. No one else gets the privilege of rendering judgment on your life in general and on your healing journey specifically. Please also remember one very important thing: absolutely *no one* is driving home from work at night, wondering if you went out on a date or booked a vacation, decided to sell the house, took off your rings, changed jobs, or anything else you have in your heart to do. Do you know why? Because after all has been said by the Energy Drainer (generally in the worst possible way), they go right back to living their life—which is fine.

It's time for you to live *your* life, *your* way. And remember Cher's wise words (tits notwithstanding): "It's nobody's business but my own."

Here's your fifth Boot Camp Affirmation. Keep it with you.

I recognize that what others think of me is not half as important as what I think of me, and my healing journey is indeed nobody's business but mine. Not everyone will agree with what I do or how I do it. However, as long as I'm not hurting myself or anyone else, and as long as I continue to fulfill my responsibilities and obligations, I will pursue my healing journey in the ways that I see fit.

Boot Camp Challenge

It is time for you to get honest with yourself. Find a quiet space and a quiet moment—no distractions allowed. Now, think of just one thing that you've really wanted to do (or try) with all of your heart but have been afraid to do or try specifically because of what someone (or several someones) might say or think. Perhaps someone has already ventured opinions that succeeded in discouraging you or stopping you altogether. This is the moment that you will take the first step toward your one thing *without* asking the opinion of anyone who isn't or hasn't been supportive of your healing journey. Got it in mind? Good. Now take just *one* tiny step toward it.

Price out that vacation (it doesn't have to be long in duration or far from home); complete that online dating profile; see what new job possibilities exist in your chosen field; begin the task of going through your beloved's things; make a decision regarding your rings (or not)—just one thing (whatever it may be) that you feel you have been prevented from doing because of the opinions of others. Those opinions no longer rule your life. It's time to put your tits on your back. Take that one tiny step right *now*.

The one thing I'd love to do/try is:

_____

_____

_____

_____

The first steps that I'm going to take toward my one thing
within the next seven days are:

_____

_____

_____

_____

How I feel after taking steps toward my one thing:

_____

_____

_____

_____

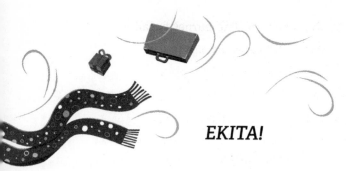

EKITA!

Loss arrives without instructions,
provides no sense of direction,
and sends everyone it touches into a sort of emotional vertigo.

❤

Loss takes the life that you built and
once knew and loved,
throws that entire life into a blender,
and then sets the blender to puree.

❤

Loss upends everything that was once familiar
and transforms it into the fearsome, strange, and unknown
in what feels to be an instant.
It takes time, patience, and grace to recover
and begin moving forward.

❤

Remember that as long as you are not coping
in a destructive manner,
There is no *right* way.
There is no *wrong* way.
There is only *your* way.

This is not one healing journey fits all—
Because it doesn't.
Yes, there is help available.
But you must tailor that help to *your* specific needs
and to *your* specific journey,
a journey that can't be compared to anyone else
and belongs to no one else.
No one.

Does One Grief
Fit All?

As you might correctly guess, I receive my fair share of invitations to grief workshops, grief conferences, grief seminars, and so forth. A few years ago, I received one such invitation, including a description of a workshop that kind of, well, horrified me.

The workshop description was as follows (in part):

Have you experienced grief?
Did you know that all grief is the same and the steps to grief
recovery are exactly the same?

Um ... *seriously?*

I was horrified and, naturally, my horrified reaction also got me to thinking. It made me think back to the old days, when pantyhose packages used to insist that "One size fits all." My reaction then was pretty much the same as it was when I saw the workshop description: "This is a joke, right?"

As I tried to absorb this ridiculous workshop description, I allowed myself to drift back in my mind. Back to a terrible season in time...

It was a rare moment of quiet during an otherwise horrendous time that had been filled with people, commotion, doctors, confusion, more doctors, tumult, and way too many opinions from way too many outsiders, most of whom had absolutely no idea what they were talking about.

Dusk was falling outside. Inside the unlit room, it was silent... almost peaceful, the idyll broken only by the invasive sounds of monitors and machines. At long last, we were alone—just the two of us. He was in a semi-comatose state, not at all conscious, yet periodically calling out in a frightened voice for his mother and one of his sisters like a scared little boy. It was heartbreaking to hear.

Believing with absolute certainty that he could hear me, I held his hand and spoke calmly to him. I stroked his arm. I kissed his cheek. I told him stories and recounted happy memories of years gone by. Over and over, I repeated that I was right there with him and reassured him that there was no reason to be afraid, that everything was going to be fine. My outward calm was an award-worthy act. My eyes brimmed over with tears that burned and slid silently down my cheeks, stubbornly defying the calm that I was trying so ardently to display. Inside, I was sobbing—heaving, wracking sobs. He was dying. I *knew* he was dying.

I knew that any hope of his surviving this bastard disease was lost. The end was approaching; ominously, stealthily, and resolutely.

I had to let go. Yet how could I let him go, when all I wanted was for him to stay? How could I possibly go on without glimpsing the twinkle in his eye? How could I live without the hugs, the corny jokes, the ritual barbecue Sundays? The absolute, undeniable, unconditional love?

Indeed, I was crying like a small child, which made perfect sense. He is, after all . . . my daddy.

I suppose this is the point where I should say, "Gotcha!" because you likely thought I was speaking of Mike. Tragically, this story is true as it is written. At that moment, I was already a grieving widow and now a grieving daughter as well. Given this set of circumstances, I'm therefore here to testify out loud and very noisily: all grief is *not* the same. I believe that to state otherwise is irresponsible.

I realize that much of our death-denying, loss-discussion-avoiding society would prefer that grief—any and all kinds of grief—was packaged nicely and neatly and wrapped up with a big black bow. In other words, all grief should be lumped together, thereby significantly shortening (or denying altogether) the necessity to grieve individual losses as what they are: *individual.*

Did I grieve the loss of my father in the same ways that I grieved the loss of my husband? Absolutely not, and with good reason: to one I was a wife, and to the other, a child. How can anyone asserting authority on the subject of loss imply that *all* losses are the same (or even parallel), and then go on to claim that the steps to *all* grief recovery are "exactly the same," regardless of the kind of loss? The complexion of grief is different, because every single loss relationship and perspective is different.

Take a moment, grab a pen, and have a quick look back over your life up to this point. Put a checkmark next to any of the following that you have lost:

- ✓ A parent
- ✓ A child
- ✓ Any family member
- ✓ A dear friend
- ✓ A pet
- ✓ A job
- ✓ A home (whether by disaster or due to financial challenge)
- ✓ A pregnancy
- ✓ A serious relationship or engagement
- ✓ A marriage (due to divorce)
- ✓ A physical capability
- ✓ Stable health
- ✓ Financial security

In addition to our spouses, most of us have lost at least one thing on that list, and *every single one* of these losses deserves to be grieved accordingly. Would you then color all of these various kinds of loss (and the subsequent grief) with the same brush? Would you grieve these losses in the exact same manner? Of course not.

Teaching that all grief is the same is essentially denying people the right to grieve each loss individually, and that's just unfair. Further, to state that all grief is the same is a polite way of saying, "Throw all of your losses into one big pile of misery, get your crying done, hurry it up, and just get over it." That's unfair too, not to mention insensitive and potentially destructive. Please hear my heart while you assert the following "get real about grief" affirmation.

I recognize that:

1. All grief is *not* the same, and, therefore, my steps to grief recovery *are not* and *will not* be the same.
2. I'm *entitled* to grieve each and every loss throughout my life as the unique losses that they are, because my loss perspectives and relationships to each loss are unique.
3. Losses are not like purchasing limits set during sales at grocery stores. I'm therefore not limited in the number of losses that I need to mourn and I will not allow *anyone* to place any such limits on me.
4. As long as I'm not coping in a destructive manner, I will grieve any and all losses in any manner that I see fit, regardless of what people around me say or think.

They were two men. I was wife to one and daughter to the other. They were two separate, distinct, and unbearably difficult losses. I recognized and grieved those two losses as such. All grief is *not* the same. And just as with the pantyhose, one grief does *not* fit all. Don't let anyone try to convince you otherwise.

EKITA!

Have you ever been unfairly judged
or feel as though you're being judged right now?
It's not a great feeling.
The next time you feel as though you're being judged,
or the next time someone makes a disparaging comment
about you, your widowhood, or your healing journey,
stop and take a really close look
at the person behind that judgment.
Then, take a really close look at yourself.
Do you see any difference at all between you
and the person who has the nerve to cast judgment?
You will.

The Epic Struggle:
Death Versus Divorce

B e it biblical or folk, fictional or popular, history in all its forms has had its share of classic struggles and conflicts: David versus Goliath, the Hatfields versus the McCoys, Billie Jean King versus Bobby Riggs, the Beatles versus the Rolling Stones, Ginger versus Mary Ann, the Dallas Cowboys versus Just About Any Other Team in the NFL, and of course, My Hair versus Humidity.

Let's look at yet another epic struggle and conflict with which countless widowed have taken serious issue:

Death versus divorce.

Many in the widowed community have encountered people who have made comments to the effect of, "I know how you feel; I'm divorced." Frankly speaking, many of those widowed have also been nearly overcome with the desire to hit these people in the head.

At one of my personal appearances, two widows shared their own stories. One widow was told by a divorced acquaintance that she was "fortunate to have a fresh start." Another heard, "You're lucky your husband died; at least you'll never have to see him again." Can you imagine? Perhaps you can.

Let's examine facts. First, a divorced person is generally dealing with some level of animosity (whether they initiated the divorce or not) and may likely prefer not ever having to see or hear from their ex-spouse again. Second (and commonly), those who have endured a divorce do see themselves as having endured a "death" of sorts: the death of a marriage, the death of the promise of a planned future, and the death of a life once shared.

Having been down the divorce road myself prior to marrying Mike, and along with anyone who has a heart, we all naturally sympathize with those who have endured or are enduring the very real pain of divorce. However, the fact remains that in a divorce situation, somebody somewhere made a choice to leave the marriage. The same cannot be said for the widowed. A widowed's marriage ended through and by no one's choosing. These marriages ended by sudden or lengthy illness, accident, tragedy, or other unforeseen circumstances—not because of somebody's choice.[1]

So how can anyone realistically compare divorce to widowhood? The answer is simple. The divorced are comparing the very real *emotional* deaths that they've experienced to the losses that widowed have endured. They see these deaths as a common denominator and great equalizer with the widowed. Moreover, and

---

1 To those who are surviving spouses of suicide victims: As discussed in Chapter Seven ("When Grieving Becomes Dangerous"), I fervently believe that your loved one did not "choose" to leave, even though the death may have been by their own hand. Remember that it is not that they necessarily wanted to leave . . . they simply could not figure out a way to stay through their pain.

just as the widowed often do, divorcees, too, are likely suffering through pain, anger, bitterness, feelings of abandonment, possible financial challenges, and an uncertain future. They then automatically assume the parallel, that they can directly relate to the widowed's feelings—and it's up to the widowed to *gently* correct them.

(Unless they say something utterly ridiculous, like the divorcee who once said to a widow, "I wish my husband would drop dead too." Or how about, "Being a widow is much easier than divorce; at least you know where your husband is." Then you have my blessing to throw the word "gently" out the window.)

A few years ago, a woman's husband was divorcing her after leaving her for a much younger woman. One can only imagine the pain and the betrayal that she must have felt, and this poor woman badly needed to talk to someone. However, posting on a social media page designed specifically for the widowed community and telling other widowed that she knew what they were going through because she had been left for a younger woman was perhaps not her wisest choice.

Predictably, this woman's post resulted in a number of unfortunate rebuttal comments made by widowed, until one of them posted a wonderful reply in response:

"While your feelings of loss are valid, divorce is not the same as being widowed. I had an acquaintance make the same analogy regarding her husband leaving her for another woman. I let her know that I did not appreciate the comparison. I am not dismissing your feelings of loss and I do feel terrible for you, but please do not assume that being widowed is similar. It would be good for you to join a divorce support group, which could really help you."

This insightful widow did a fantastic job of educating our divorced friend by *gently* letting her know that, while no one is dismissive or uncaring of how she rightfully feels; she should none-theless realize that loss of a spouse is not the same as divorce from a spouse. The losses are separate, distinct . . . and incomparable.

While you may not understand how anyone could make the sort of comments that were made to these widowed (because I certainly don't understand it), it is nonetheless up to the widowed commu-nity to let the divorced know that while we definitely appreciate the fact that they, too, have suffered a heart-crushing loss and that we are absolutely sympathetic to that loss, the intangible deaths that accompany divorce can't be compared on any level to actual spousal loss. The widowed should feel free to correct anyone who is trying to draw comparisons between divorce and loss. Not by playing a game of "My Pain is Worse than Your Pain" as discussed earlier, but by gently stating that death is simply not the same as divorce; that you are not "lucky" to have lost your spouse or "fortu-nate" to have a "fresh start" in any way, shape, or form. While each is life-altering in their own right, death and divorce cannot and should not ever be compared.

EKITA!

One of the biggest and most understandable
complaints from the bereaved
is that the people who surround them expect
(and occasionally demand) them
to recover from their loss very quickly.
In fact, too quickly.
Unreasonably quickly.
But are *you* guilty of the same thing?

❤

Do *you* expect yourself to heal and move forward from
unbelievable, mind-numbing, life-altering, core-shaking loss and grief
in the time that it takes to defrost tonight's dinner?
Before you can expect others around you to treat you
in the way that you deserve to be treated,
you must first honestly recognize the enormity
of what you have been through
and that from which you are recovering.

Bereavement
Boot Camp Lesson Six:
Get Up, Get Moving, Get *Out!*

I t is time for Boot Camp Lesson Six. Have you noticed any changes in your healing journey at this point? I hope so, because I'm now about to push you right out of your house. Did I just give you a big headache? I wouldn't be surprised if your answer is "Yes," because I know that at one time, the thought of leaving the house, socializing, or being in public in any way at all made me want to crawl under the covers with a large order of fried something from a drive-thru.[1]

We've spent a decent amount of publishing real estate discussing Energy Drainers and how they don't have a place on your healing journey—which is the truth. It's now time to turn full attention to your Energy *Givers*, the person or people in your life without

---

1 ... with a bucket-sized Coca-Cola. Regular ... not diet.

whom you would feel lost. All of your wonderful Energy Givers have one real need in common and it's a very strong need, that of putting their collective arms around you to show their love and support in any and all ways possible. It's up to you to help them fulfill this sincere need by permitting them to give you love and support in the ways that they are able.

Many who are grieving complain that people aren't there for them during difficult times—but are you actually *allowing* people to be there for you? Be honest. How many invitations to dinner or shopping or coffee have you turned down? Have you declined offers of help (either at work or at home) in favor of telling people that you're "fine"? When someone volunteers to bring dinner over or run the kids or get you out of the house for a walk, have you once accepted? If the answer to any of the above is no, it is now time to let people *in.*

I know. At a time of loss or life challenge, many of us would rather just disappear from public view and turn inward, rather than even think about social interaction. I completely get that because it all seems an exhaustive effort: getting ready to go someplace, actually *going* to that someplace, and then feeling like you have to be all smiles and on your game . . . when you may very well be feeling like you have no game to be "on" in the first place.

Many of you may already be familiar with this story. Less than one month after Mike's death, I was scheduled to attend a business conference in Dallas involving approximately 10,000 attendees. At that point, I had just lost Mike, survived his funeral (not to mention the over-three-year journey that was his diagnostic process and illness), and had somehow gotten through Hanukah, Christmas, and New Year's (though I can't remember much about any of it). As you can imagine, a conference of this (or any) magnitude was obviously the very last thing in which I wanted to participate. I loved my work and my colleagues with whom I shared that work; however (and speaking truthfully), the thought of traveling halfway across the country and having to paste on the "face" that we all paste on at one time or another just made my head hurt. To be honest, I don't think I was even out of my pajamas at that point.

I was firm in my decision to stay home from the conference, when I received a call from a colleague who was not only an amazing mentor to me, she was also very much a part of our family's journey throughout Mike's illness. She called in an effort to convince me to attend the conference. Now, keep in mind that several others had previously attempted to exercise their powers of persuasion and had all failed. Amazing mentor or otherwise, I was not about to be dissuaded from my very stubborn decision to stay at home, in my pajamas, with all of the blinds closed.

After listening to my various and oft-repeated protestations, this beautiful woman finally said, "Carole, there are so many of us who couldn't get to the funeral[2] and we want to put our arms around you and share in your sorrow. Please come and let us lift you."

It was then that I realized that those who cared for me, and who were such an integral part of my journey to that point, now needed to be able to both express their love and support me through my grieving process as I began my healing journey. I then realized that it would have been otherwise selfish to deny this opportunity to those who truly cared so much, so I eventually chose to attend the

---

2 Mike's funeral took place four days before Christmas and while most of the United States was buried under severe blizzards. One can understand the inability to travel.

conference. Although I was obviously subdued throughout the conference and there was more crying than laughing on my part, I am so very grateful that I allowed my own wonderful Energy Givers to be a part of the infancy of my healing journey, when, otherwise left to my own devices, I would have stayed home.

After the conference, I began accepting invitations: a quiet dinner with friends, a movie with a girlfriend, a glass of wine and appetizers at a friend's house, occasional events at my synagogue. These were all activities that were well within my comfort zone and that not only made me feel better but also allowed my inner circle of Energy Givers to be a part of a healing process in which *they* needed to participate—after all, they, too, had suffered a loss.

You must be willing to allow your Energy Givers the opportunity to lift you and be proactive and useful participants in your healing journey. This allowance obviously does not have to be at a conference with thousands of people or at a huge party or at a club, which can definitely be overwhelming. However, a lunch or coffee with a close friend is not at all difficult. Or how about a movie? Crowds are generally at a minimum during an afternoon matinee or a late showing, and you can enjoy a couple of hours of light entertainment (not to mention sinfully wonderful movie-theater popcorn) with someone who wants oh-so-much to help you feel better— if only for a little while.

I acknowledge and agree that you absolutely have every right to be quiet and introspective. However, you also need the support and the reinforcement of the people who truly love you and want nothing more for you than your healthy recovery. These same people need to be able to be a part of that recovery process. Don't push that support—or these fantastic people—away.

In attempting to educate the public away from saying things like "Call me if you need anything" (because we all know that simply doesn't happen), I instead provide ideas as to what people can actually do for someone in the throes of sorrow or difficulty. The suggestions always include taking proactive measures; however, proactivity takes two parties—and your Energy Givers' proactivity is not going to help at all if you choose not to accept it. It's kind of like a forward pass in a football game—all of the quarterback talent and throwing accuracy in the world does not mean a damn thing if the receivers aren't catching the ball. In other words, be a receiver. It's time for you to catch the ball.

Here's your sixth Boot Camp Affirmation. Keep it with you:

> My healing journey is not only about my grief or my needs alone.
> There are those around me who are willing and eager to help me.
> For that reason, even though I may not necessarily be feeling social
> or even feel like leaving the house for anything other than work and
> other obligations, I will endeavor to begin accepting invitations for
> quiet social activities. I will also accept offers of practical help, under-
> standing that permitting others to help me is an important part of
> their healing process.

Boot Camp Challenge

Whether it's to go out for a couple of hours to enjoy a meal or movie or to someone's home for a cup of coffee, accept just *one* invitation. That's it. Say *yes* to just *one* of those invitations. Then actually *go*—no cancelling allowed. If you find that you're up to accepting more than one invitation, by all means do so, but if you feel that this might be overwhelming, go back to choosing just one invitation. In the alternative, accept just *one* offer of help that you have received—offers to help with errands, with housekeeping, with children, with meals, or any other kind offers of help that come your way. Pick just one of those offers and accept it.

I have accepted invitations from:

Name	Activity	How I felt afterward

I have accepted offers of help from:

Name	Helped with	How I felt afterward

EKITA!

Remember that you can and should integrate the memories and
beauty of your previous life with your loved one
into your new life now.
Your heart will expand infinitely to accept new love into your life,
without limitation and regardless of what that "new love" looks like.
In other words, whether you've fallen in love with

a new home

a new career

a new hobby or pastime

a new place

a new person

a new direction in life

a new "you"

some of the above

or all of the above and then some . . .

Don't let anyone make you feel guilty about it.

Including *you.*

You aren't dishonoring, casting aspersion upon, or disrespecting the
memory of your loved one or the life that you lived together.

You are simply embracing the fact

—and the reality—

that by being here, you deserve everything that life has to offer you and whatever it is that you seek.

And that includes your happiness and your peace.

CHAPTER
20

Depression:
You Don't Have to Do It Alone

Here comes a tough question that again requires absolute honesty on your part. Are you now or have you been battling depression since the loss of your spouse? Have you ever felt like something was wrong with you because you are battling feelings of depression? Take another travel back in time with me . . .

About three months prior to his death, Mike lost the ability to safely chew and swallow food, another horrible hallmark of ALS. Subsequently, surgeons placed a feeding tube in him so he could safely and comfortably receive nutrition. Once he was home from the hospital after the procedure, he was initially fed by an infusion pump (which looks like a clunky, bulkier version of an IV) that was equipped with a startlingly loud alarm,[1] which was primed to sound

---

1 Imagine a car alarm going off in your living room. It will get your attention.

should any part of the machinery malfunction. The at-home nurs-
ing instructor showed me the intricacies of the machinery and how
to change and navigate the various nutrient-filled bags, while Mike
had *that* look on his face to which I had become so accustomed . . .
the look that clearly said, "I'm just so *over* this." Who could blame
him?

As cruel fate would have it, the infusion machine did indeed malfunction, and it naturally chose to do so at 2:30 AM, setting off the
aforementioned startling alarms, both on the machine and in our
heart rhythms. It being the middle of the night and as one might
expect, I could not get anyone on the phone to help me. I finally had
to call the 911 operator, who sent paramedics to our house to correct
the malfunctioning pump and re-establish the infusion lines. All in
all, the result was one very unpleasant slumber party for the two
of us.

Having had absolutely no real sleep for several consecutive days,
and as most of our bodies do when we're not taking proper care of
ourselves, my own body chose the day after the machinery malfunction to retaliate against me with another terrible episode of
shingles, so bad that I was bleeding from the backs of my legs. Factor
in that it was ninety-five degrees, our home had no air conditioning,
and our entire family had been in this terrible battle against ALS
for over two years, suffice it to say, none of us were doing very well.

As fate would have it, the machine again malfunctioned. As I
resumed my wrestling match with the uncooperative infusion
machinery (still insistently sounding alarms every fifteen minutes)
while simultaneously wiping the blood from my shingle-ridden
legs and trying to keep Mike cool from the terrible heat, the façade
finally cracked. I began to cry. Uncontrollably. Unabashedly. As he

watched me crumble like month-old bread, Mike was understandably worried. When he asked what was wrong, I blurted, "I think I'm depressed."

He nodded understandingly and sympathetically, of course, while I immediately felt incredibly guilty at my impulsive admission. Talk about selfishness. Where did *I* get off complaining about depression? After all, *he* was the one who was dying. So from that day forward, I kept quiet. I squashed the "feels." I didn't say another word about feeling depressed—to Mike or to anyone else.

Not long after Mike's death, I confessed to my mother the deep, dark secret that I had long been harboring. I finally revealed that I "might be depressed"—and then I immediately apologized to her for saying it. She looked at me with a raised eyebrow and said, "Well, let's see, you've just lost your husband after two years of illness. You've just undergone major surgery, and your father is in a coma. You 'think' you're depressed? Carole, you would be weird if you *weren't* depressed."

I felt more freedom in hearing those words than I'd felt in a very long time. Imagine the relief at discovering that there was not anything "wrong" with me! I was not being selfish, nor was I losing my precariously balanced marbles. My husband had died; my own physical health was at an all-time ebb; my father had just been declared terminally ill—and apparently, it was perfectly fine to be depressed about *all* of it.

At what point did so many people (including the widowed themselves) begin to believe that we should not be depressed or sad or at the very least perhaps a little quieter than usual? Stop and think about what you have been through:

The loss of a spouse

The adjustments that you've had to make as a result

The inevitable challenges that you've faced

The myriad post-loss chores that require attention

Trying to re-establish routine in a household that must continue in spite of everything

The obligations of a job

Is it any wonder that you are not feeling quite like yourself?

If you are now or have been feeling depressed since the loss of your beloved, I'm delighted to let you know that just as I was, you, too, are absolutely 100 percent normal in having those feelings. I recently heard a statement that I thought was absolutely spot-on:

> "Sadness is when you care about everything . . . depression is when you care about nothing."

Is it normal to feel depressed during and after the experience called widowhood? Without question. However, there is a huge difference between depression that lasts for a finite period of time in reaction to a traumatic event and depression that takes over, permeates, and dominates your entire life. It's incredibly vital to make the distinction between situational depression and a depression that's causing an inability not only to function in your daily life but eventually to thrive again. As I am so fond of saying, you don't have to do your grief all by yourself. If you need help, *please* get help!

Broken Heart Syndrome: It *Is* a Thing

We have all seen the stories many times. A couple who were married for decades die within days, hours, or even minutes of each other. Siblings who enjoyed a deep bond throughout their lives pass away in shockingly close proximity to one another. A news story tells of a gentleman who died less than twenty-four hours after his beloved fifteen-year-old dog was euthanized due to cancer. I myself recall when a colleague's husband passed away at a very young age after a battle with brain cancer . . . and the day after the funeral, his father suddenly died as well.

Our collective reactions to these heartstring-tugging stories are largely similar. We either cluck sympathetically or pragmatically wonder at the marvel and mystery of "coincidence." However, a closer examination of many of these types of stories has yielded an emerging and tragic truth. Suffering from a broken heart after a loss is not a mere figure of speech meant to reference only emotional trauma. There exists an actual, serious, *physical* affliction called broken heart syndrome,[2] an affliction that can unfortunately result in devastating consequences.

We are all well aware of the effects that stress has on our overall health. As Mike's illness rapidly progressed, I quickly went from being a vital, energetic, extremely active, and healthy woman, to suffering a dramatic increase in the frequency and severity of once-occasional migraine headaches. Previously visiting only every couple of years, colds and flu viruses were attacking me frequently—my immune system no longer had the ability to fight them off, and I was constantly sick. Most telling about the toll that the overwhelming stress was taking on my physical health was my first bout with shingles, typically considered to be an "older person" virus,[3] and that once "awakened" does not disappear.

---

2 Source: The American Heart Association: "Is Broken Heart Syndrome Real?" *www.heart.org.*

3 I was thirty-nine years old . . . and even though the degree of severity varies from episode to episode, shingles will likely recur throughout the rest of your life. Which is also not fun.

Given the obvious and very real impact that stress can have on a person's body, shouldn't it logically follow that depression and/or severe emotional stress might physically impact the heart as well? It should, but apparently logic has taken time to catch up with fact.

Whether examined from a medical or a layperson standpoint, broken heart syndrome makes a great deal of sense. Just as the rest of the body can be compromised by extraordinary stress, so, too, can the heart. The heart is just as capable of going into shock as the rest of the body; except when a heart goes into shock, it can be fatal. The unfortunate part is that too many people (and women in particular) either assume that potential cardiac symptoms are due to something else (indigestion, food poisoning, flu, fatigue, a bad day . . . or overwhelming grief) and either self-medicate or simply ignore the symptoms altogether. In fact, it is only in recent years that the medical community acknowledged and now educates that cardiac symptoms in women can manifest much differently than in men, and that those symptoms can again vary widely from woman to woman.

Further, and in a sad double-down on a situation with a potentially tragic outcome, many who may be suffering from broken heart syndrome may also be surrounded by people with dismissive or less-than-enlightened attitudes—the people who say things like, "It's all in your head," or, "You just need to get some sleep," or any similar phrase that trivializes someone else's pain. The problem here is twofold. First, we know that emotional trauma can have serious physical effects. Worse, the person who is being told "Get over it," or "It's about time you stopped crying," may then ignore any physical symptoms that they are experiencing, instead convincing themselves that their symptoms are all in their head because someone else (whose salutation likely is not "Doctor") told them so.

Now, if you don't experience any physical symptoms or issues after a loss or trauma, does it mean that your heart isn't "broken?" Of course not. Your heart, your spirit, your soul, and your psyche are most definitely broken in the emotional sense, and dramatic physical events, afflictions, or infirmities are not prerequisites to experiencing the anguish of raw grief. However, what can no longer be ignored, trivialized, or swept under the rug is this:

> Broken heart syndrome is not only a real thing, it also has the potential to kill.

Remember that a symptom—*any* symptom—is simply your body trying to tell you something—and it's your obligation to *listen to what your body is telling you*. Therefore, in addition to any potential cardiac symptoms, you must immediately contact your doctor (or 911 and/or your local emergency room) if you experience *any* of the following:

- ✓ Dizziness
- ✓ Heart palpitations or arrhythmia
- ✓ Chest pain and/or severe upper or middle-back pain
- ✓ Headaches
- ✓ Nausea/vomiting
- ✓ Fatigue (to the point that you're unable to work or otherwise function normally)
- ✓ Digestive problems or any inability to properly assimilate food
- ✓ Inability to sleep

✓ Sudden hair loss

✓ Serious loss of or unusual increase in appetite

✓ Sudden/rapid weight loss or weight gain

✓ Fear/anxiety (that interferes with or prevents adequate nutrition, rest, and ability to function)

✓ Feelings of hopelessness or despair

✓ Suicidal ideation

✓ *Any* other symptom(s) that appear suddenly and/or you know to be atypical for you

Please *don't ever ignore any symptoms* that you experience post trauma, be they physical, emotional, or mental. Do not be embarrassed to acknowledge and/or share your symptoms. Do not try to convince yourself that, "This too will pass; it's all in my head and I'm just sad." Do *not* let anyone around you trivialize or minimize what you are feeling, or tell you that yours is simply a "get over it" situation. Broken heart syndrome *is* real. If you (or someone you know) need help, please reach out for help. Right *now*.

Give Peace (of Mind) a Chance

There are fantastic mental health professionals who are ready and eager to help you get through this terrible season in your life. They can also help you distinguish if yours is a situational depression or if you are suffering from possible clinical depression.

You might be thinking, *Well, Carole, I tried counseling* (or therapy or treatment or books or support groups) *and it did no good, so I quit.* I equate that to saying, *Well, I tried this antibiotic for my sore throat and it didn't do any good, so I'm not taking medicine anymore.* If the medicine that I am taking for the sore throat is not working, I talk to my doctor and I change medications. The same principle applies here. If whatever you tried or whomever you saw didn't work for you, try something or someone else! If one book failed to speak to your grief or did not adequately resonate with you, get another book—and another and another. Try a different support group or treatment or counselor or therapist. Talk honestly to your doctor, your therapist, your cleric: *anyone* who is in a position of caring and compassion that can either help you directly or get you to the help you need.

Always remember . . . it doesn't have to hurt forever. You do *not* have to do this alone.

EKITA!

Not every day is going to be positive.

Not every person who crosses your path is going to be positive,

and not every outcome to every situation is going to be

what you're seeking or what you deserve.

However, while we can't necessarily control life circumstances,

we can choose how to both approach those circumstances

and our reactions to those circumstances.

Why not approach our days and our healing journeys with positive

expectancy?

❤

Do you have a positive expectancy?

Do you have a positive outlook?

Have you taken positive measures or steps to take you

in the directions you wish to go?

If not, now is a great time to start.

❤

If a negative comes your way,

that's okay.

Get really angry,

deal with it,

reset to positive,

and go forward.

Grief Shaming: The Latest Form of Bereavement Judgment

Blame it on the relatively recent ability to remain anonymous, on people who have very little lives, or a combination thereof. In recent years, there has been a sharp increase in varying sorts of public "shaming": weight shaming (be it over or under), height shaming, financial shaming, social status shaming, a certain kind of shaming that questions sexual conduct (real or imagined and generally reserved exclusively for women), or shaming just for the sheer and pathetic "sport" of it. The Internet in general and social media in particular are popular avenues on which to indulge in such shaming—and one need only visit the "Comments" section of most online media outlets, websites, or social media hubs to confirm this observation. If further proof beyond comment sections was necessary, I recently ran across an online article entitled

"Twenty Celebrities Who Have Ugly Spouses." Point illustrated.

It therefore saddens me to have to add one more form of sham-ing to this rapidly-mushrooming list: grief shaming.

Many find a great deal of comfort in visiting the gravesites or memorial sites of their departed loved ones—and that's a won-derful thing. Some visit to experience quiet reflection and feel connected to their beloved, while others invite friends for picnics, remembrances, or even mini-celebrations. There is no doubt that visiting the gravesite of a loved one can bring a large measure of peace and consolation to those coping with the pain of loss.

I am not among those people.

When it comes to my own healing journey, I find my comfort in the happy memories of Mike when he was energetically healthy and vital. I picture him completely free of the ravages of the illness that savaged his body and stole him from this life. I envision him on the back of a horse, wearing his standard "uniform," consisting of a crisply triple-starched Western shirt, perfectly creased jeans, and a Stetson hat. I envision Mike and my daddy (who passed away four months after Mike) regaling one another with boring stories over cold beer and barbecue, as they so often loved to do. My comfort comes from the glimmers of Mike that I see in Kendall, an ado-lescent when her daddy passed away and now a young woman, whose language and expressions are ever-so-slightly tinged with his inflections.[1] In my heart, in my mind, and in my own place of peace, Mike doesn't lie in a grave—and it is for that reason that I

---

1 Especially when she's angry, which is actually pretty funny.

don't visit. His gravesite is simply not a place of tranquility for me. I realize that this particular confession may elicit raised eyebrows; however, as I do in kind, I continue to strongly encourage anyone experiencing bereavement of any sort to seek their comfort and peace in their own specific ways and by their own design.

All of that said, would I *ever* deign to influence another person to find their comfort in the exact same ways as I, or worse, shame another for seeking comfort in ways they see fit? Never.

What is disturbing are those people who feel the need or the entitlement to dictate exactly *how* others should be expressing their grief and seeking comfort. If those expressions of grief don't fall precisely in line with these generally unsolicited opinions, it is somehow indicative of the love (or alleged lack thereof) that a survivor feels for their beloved.

Can you imagine the pain and the guilt that one widow felt when she was asked, "Why don't you ever visit his grave? Didn't you love him?" Or the utter confusion of a widower who visits his late wife's grave once a week and was eventually confronted with, "Why are you spending all of your time at the cemetery?" How bewildered one widow must have been when she was chastised by friends for simply going to a movie two months after her husband's death. And just imagine the overwhelming guilt that another widow felt after she shared that she'd gone on her first post-loss date two years after her husband's passing, and was subsequently asked, "How does it feel to dance on your husband's grave?"[2]

All of these scenarios—and too many more to list—are perfect illustrations of grief shaming. And the unfortunate result of grief

---

2 I was the widow on the receiving end of that last remark.

shaming is that the bereaved willingly absorb both the negativity and the shame, winding up feeling even *more* grief, guilt, doubt, fear, and uncertainty than that with which they are already coping.

Grief shaming—the questions, opinions, and admonishments that are set upon the bereaved either publicly or otherwise—is nothing more than code for, "You aren't grieving in the exact manner as I either am or believe that I might; therefore, you're grieving 'incorrectly' and 'inappropriately,' and you should be ashamed of yourself." In other words, because your grief perspective is unique to you, the actions that you're taking, whatever they may be, are judged to be wrong or inappropriate or some other ill-advised adjective. Once questioned (or accused) as to the manner in which the grieving pursue their comfort, too many once again find themselves in those places of pain, guilt, doubt, fear, and/or writing letters that begin with the phrase, "Is it okay if I do/don't . . ." or, "Is it appropriate to/not to. . . ." These letters subsequently continue with the part of the healing journey that's being questioned, opined upon, or outright judged.

Although I've repeated the same words countless times to what are now many thousands of people, and you've been given this message a number of times throughout the book, I again gently remind you that your healing journey is yours *alone.* As long as you're not coping with your grief in a destructive manner (and you now have a clearly defined knowledge as to what destructive coping entails), however you choose to grieve, seek support, find solace, pursue your life post-loss, and ultimately heal is *your* choice. No other person on this planet can tell you how to feel, how to grieve, and most importantly, how you should or should not be pursuing whatever brings you comfort, peace, and happiness.

Those indulging in the exercise of grief shaming are not living *your* life. They're not the ones left behind to slowly and surely find a way forward into a new life post-loss. Seek comfort in *your* unique way, regardless of the opinions of anyone around you. Remember, these people *are not you*. Find your peace wherever and however you wish, and revel in the warmth of your treasured memories rather than with those who choose to be anything less than supportive of you and your goal of ultimate healing.

In other words, no grief shaming allowed.

EKITA!

The people who can't figure out why
you're not "better" yet
are usually the same people who assume that as it
may have with them,
the mere passage of time will lessen your grief.

❤

In reality, there is only one widowed person:
You.
And *no one else* will feel this loss
in the same ways that you do.

❤

Many people don't realize
that throughout a healing journey,
there are numerous grief "triggers" and grief "re-visits"
that will come your way.

❤

Don't heed others who may be trying to dictate a
healing timeline to you,
because the timeline that they want you to use
is the timeline that belongs to *them*.

♥

Instead . . .
accept any grief triggers or re-visits that come your way;
pay close and honest attention to how you're feeling
in the triggered moment.
Honor and embrace those feelings accordingly,
and take peace in knowing
that your forward-focused healing journey
will continue once again.

CHAPTER 22

Sorrow and Social Media: The Side the Scientists Don't See

C onfession time yet again: I am a blonde-haired, green-eyed, modern-day dinosaur. There once was a time when to me, "high tech" was a lava lamp and interior design included a bean bag chair and a blacklight. I've made each reluctant move from vinyl records to cassette tapes to CDs to digital download and streaming that rapidly mushrooming technology demanded of me. I lingered as long as possible with VHS technology, and rather than make the (again reluctant and long overdue) move to a DVR, preferred instead to race home from wherever I was in time to see the shows that I wanted to see or hit the "record" button. Oh, and I miss flip phones.

Suffice it to say, I was dragged kicking and screaming into the wonder that has become social media. Even after my administrative assistant relocated our online community onto Facebook, I still refused to join. It wasn't until years later (and after a great deal of shaming on the part of said administrative assistant and my daughter) that I, too, became a part of the social media cybersphere.

What I didn't realize at that time was that social media had the capacity to be an incredible instrument in grief recovery. I had delighted in watching thousands of friendships form through our own website message boards, and social media took that potential to entirely new levels. Our community grew rapidly and, consequently, so did the ability to reach many more people in need of grief recovery education and support. People not only participated on various community pages, they also began creating memorial pages (or converting existing social media pages into memorial pages) that allowed others to reach out in sympathy. The shared memories, photographs, videos, and other remembrances were clearly helping the bereaved in their recovery processes.

So, it was with more than a little skepticism that I read an article wherein a British scientist declared that social media was, in fact, "making it harder to move on from heartache."[1]

Harder to move on? Having seen firsthand all of the positivity that results from being a part of an online community of healing, and marveling at the countless number of friendships that blossomed as a result, this was a theory that was difficult for me to embrace. Intrigued, I continued reading:

> Discussing how cyber culture affects the grieving process, one
> of Britain's leading scientists, [Professor] Sir Nigel Shadbolt said:

---

1 Excerpted from "Why Facebook Pictures Mean the Pain of a Bad Break-up or Losing a Loved One Doesn't Fade Like It Used To," *The Daily Mail* (United Kingdom, online, September 28, 2013).

"When bad, sad or indifferent things happened to us, over time you forgot. That is why time could be a great healer. But if you've got this complete authentic playback of people and episodes, it'll be quite haunting."

Forgot? Forgot *what?* A person lost? A life lived? Playbacks of memories are "haunting?" Feeling my crankiness level quickly escalate and trying desperately not to envision my dearly departed loved ones as characters from the "Thriller" video, I continued reading:

"And rather than being a comfort, Sir Norman [sic] suggests lingering online photos and messages can actually cause more distress. He added: 'One of the things that human psychology has evolved to do is forgetting. We don't have perfect recall, we didn't used to have this way of things being represented back to us.'"

It's true: we don't have perfect recall, and, in fact, I've long taught that we tend to have selective amnesia when it comes to actively remembering our late beloveds. We also have selective amnesia in many other areas of our lives; otherwise, the women of the world would each have one child and stop there.[2] That said, I have spent years teaching that healing and moving forward post-loss does not and should not equal forgetting. The good professor appears to feel otherwise, as though the mere passage of time is equivalent to a good and necessary dose of amnesia. The reality? The overall message being conveyed in this article is borderline dangerous to those who may already be questioning the "rights" and "wrongs" of their grief recovery.

---

2 Selective amnesia pretty much dulls the entire labor, child-bearing, and recovery process.

Further, and begging the good professor's pardon, what about the people who don't have any means of support, other than what is available to them on the Internet? What becomes of those in small towns and/or those without a readily available community? Social media might be their only means of reaching out in a meaningful and productive way. As reluctant as I may have been at one time to become a part of it, I will never deny the tremendous good that social media does to both grow and serve a community that, a little over a decade ago, simply didn't exist in cohesive form.

The debate over social media and its usefulness in general continues and there are portions of that debate with which I agree. I suppose I'll never understand someone taking to any form of social media to share that they ate an apple, went to the post office, or wash what previously would have been coined "dirty laundry" in a very public way. [3] However, if the professor (and any other experts alongside him) feels that social media is doing a collective disservice to the bereaved community, that people would be better served by allowing the mere passage of time to enable forgetting (and we all know better, right?), and that various posted remembrances ultimately hinder the healing process and do more harm than good, I would heartily invite the professor and his colleagues to speak with any one of the millions of people who've been helped as a direct result of social media interactivity. I would happily share stories of the infinite friendships formed on various online bereavement groups (ours among them) that have been built to last a lifetime, most of which would not exist absent the Internet. If people do

---

3 Please understand that I'm of the generation who shared their innermost secrets in handwritten form with well-worn diaries that came with a lock and key. Social media (along with certain so-called reality television programs) seems to have erased the need to keep private matters private.

feel hindered, held back, or stuck altogether in their healing processes because of their active participation in social media or by facilitating a page in memoriam, the answer is simple. They will remove themselves from social media of their own volition and thereafter do whatever it is that they feel will move them forward, and not because they've been told that their actions "can actually cause more distress."

I understand that grief must be continually studied and examined by the scientific and medical communities. I also understand that the societal complexion of grief and how we both view and treat the bereaved is a paradigm that is constantly shifting, perhaps never more than in the last two decades. However, and with no disrespect meant toward or directed at medical experts, scientists, academia or others who would attempt to reduce grief to solely methodical study, healing in no way equals forgetting—nor should it. To imply otherwise is sending a sorry and potentially perilous message to the bereaved community. Already generally dealing with a tremendous amount of guilt for even so much as laughing out loud after the loss of a loved one, why would anyone even suggest that moving forward equals (or worse, requires) forgetting?

The bereaved are capable of both healing after loss while carrying precious memories forward. If we teach that healing equals forgetting, or conversely, forgetting equals healing, who then is going to choose to focus on healing? Who then is going to be able to move forward without feeling guilty or feeling as though they have to "forget" in order to heal? If social media as a whole and the virtual presence of others who understand can help facilitate this process in a healthy way, who would argue that?

I have nursed and buried a husband, and shortly thereafter nursed and buried my father. I went through the paralyzing, mind-numbing grief that both losses brought, and helped Kendall to do the same. I also eventually moved forward into a new life, which includes remarriage and my wonderfully blended family. I have indeed healed; however, I have not forgotten—and I never will.

As much as the scientific world may wish it were otherwise, grief and its attendant healing process doesn't fit nicely and neatly into tidy, prefixed, scientifically sound packages. Social media can play an integral part in healing, and there needs to be greater understanding of this reality on a much wider level. Rather than inferring or outright teaching a mythical formula to the effect that healing equals forgetting, that one is prerequisite to the other, and that social media is an impediment to grief recovery, let's instead support whatever healthy and productive measures the bereaved wish to take to facilitate healing. It may not be the most scientific approach . . . but it certainly does appear to be an approach that works for too many to be disparaged or ignored.

EKITA!

As much as we would wish it otherwise,
we can't control life and death.
However, we *can* choose to control what *is*
reasonably within our control—
like our own lives.

♥

Making the choice to assume control results
in one wonderful thing:
Freedom.
Freedom from any guilt that you may feel in
connection with your beloved's death
or the circumstances surrounding their death.
Freedom from trying to live your life according to the
opinions of those who surround you.
Freedom from feeling as though healing and
moving forward from loss
automatically equals the need to forget or otherwise
walk away from memories.
Freedom from anything and anyone that may be
holding you back, dragging you down,
or bringing negativity into your space.

♥

Control is a big word and assuming control—
really assuming it—is a big step.
When you make the choice to assume control over
that which you do have control,
the peace that you rightly deserve will envelop your life.

♥

It's your life after all.
Say *yes* to controlling it.

23

Doing Social Safely: The Do's and Don'ts of Social Media

N ow that I have sung the praises of social media's positive role in grief recovery, let's explore other aspects of social media: the good, the bad, and the *really* ugly.

As you learned in the last chapter, the advent of social media has done and continues to do many wonderful things for us and the world in which we live. In addition to aiding in grief recovery for millions of people, social media has also succeeded in shrinking our globe to the point that we can "meet" fantastic new people who live anywhere and everywhere, both within and outside of the widowed community.

However, it's a sad fact that where there is good to be found in cyberspace, there is generally also bad—potentially *very* bad—lurking in the cybershadows. As much of an asset as it can be, social media is unfortunately also fraught with scammers and predators. If you're not vigilant, these parasites can easily and quickly worm their way into your life, your heart, and even your checkbook before you realize that something is not right, let alone horribly wrong.

There are many social media platforms, however, the most commonly used currently are Facebook, Twitter, and Instagram. Each has their own policies and policing tactics to help keep you safe; however, the large part of that responsibility falls to you. Many users don't realize how vulnerable they are to fake and scam accounts, organizations, and predators seeking the vulnerable, the grief-stricken, or those who are naïve about social media. Because I've witnessed far too many widowed become victims in social media arenas, and in the interest of keeping you as safe as humanly possible, permit me to share my own social media protections that I use to keep myself and my family safe and secure.

Beware the Profile Overshare

An unfortunate aspect of social media is the tendency to over-share, or what's more comically known as TMI (Too Much Information). Sometimes, TMI is merely worthy of eye-rolling (do we *really* need to share unfortunate bathroom experiences?), while other TMIs can be downright dangerous.[1]

Always remember that the more profile details you post about yourself, the more exposed you become, and the more attention you are likely to garner. When creating a profile on social media, keep in mind the following:

---

1 If you're already on social media, consider this a friendly reminder to check your social media profiles and privacy settings.

✓ Just because a question is asked or a blank space begs for information doesn't mean that you are obligated to provide that information. For example, posting your birth *date* is fine, but keep the year of your birth to yourself. List your native hometown if you wish, but think twice about listing where you currently live—and never provide your residential street address. The same goes for providing your telephone number to these sites, many of whom have experienced hacking issues. These precautions alone greatly reduce the chances of identity theft being committed against you—a crime that continues to rise with the help of information voluntarily provided on social media.

✓ Another area in which to exercise caution is that of marital status. Many widowed will list themselves accordingly, and, of course, there is nothing wrong with that. However, be aware that doing so tends to invite dubious "friend requests" and followers—which means that what I refer to as your BS radar will need to be on high alert all the time. Further, once you list yourself as widowed, you may be inviting attention that, while perhaps sincere, may not be the kind of attention that you desire. For that reason alone, there are widowed who choose to keep their status as "married," which offers slightly greater protection. You can also choose to list no marital status.

✓ Hold the rest of your personal information close to the vest, especially when it comes to where you are physically located. For example, including what you do for a living is fine; however, do not share the name, address, telephone number, etc., of your workplace.

✓ *Please* be smart with your profile pictures, cover pictures, and, for that matter, *any* pictures that you post on the Internet. In my workshops, I teach that, whether in social media or on an online dating website, your profile picture is your "cyber handshake," your first impression and a message that you're essentially sending out to the world. What impression do you wish to create? What message do you wish to send? Posting photos that are fun and show you off in your best light are great, and you'll receive sincere compliments. However . . .

Ladies: Posting pictures of yourself in lingerie or a thong bikini or pictures that show way too much skin or show you beer bonging or are otherwise potentially inappropriate, are sending messages that you really do not want to be sending. Rather than sincere compliments, you will instead be receiving sincere propositions (and worse).

Gentlemen: I love you guys—really I do—but taking a picture of yourself wrapped only in a bath towel that is shot with your cell phone in your bathroom is gross and creepy. You'd be shocked at the number of men who do just that. *All* of you have at least one friend. Get out of the bathroom, put some clothes on, hand your buddy the cell phone, and smile.

Beware the Everyday Overshare

I have two separate pages on Facebook. One is my professional "Carole Brody Fleet" author page that serves the widowed community with hot-topic discussions, keeps people up-to-date on personal and media appearances, book and article releases, and all things professional (and I hope that you'll join us on that page). The other page is my personal page for family and friends. While I obviously include work events on my personal page, it is also the page where you'll find pictures of my family, my cats, my travels, and the occasional cobb salad or lemon-drop martini. What you *won't* find on my personal page is the oversharing of anything that might endanger the security and safety of myself, my family members, or otherwise put me into a position of vulnerability.

Write It Once, Check It Twice—at Least

I've seen so many people take to Facebook to gripe about their jobs and/or their bosses—only to find themselves fired the next day. People going through divorces or civil litigation post specifics about their cases that could very well jeopardize the outcome. Proud parents post pictures of their young children along with the name and whereabouts of the schools they attend, all but sending a beacon out to predators. People spew vitriol and hatred, only to again find themselves fired from jobs (or expelled from school or even disowned by family members). One very famous account of oversharing involves a celebrity who learned a very difficult lesson when one overshares details regarding their abundant wealth.[2]

Prior to sharing anything on social media, be sure to take these steps:

1) **Set your privacy settings and review those settings regularly.** You have complete control over who can see your posts; you can even control who sees *specific* posts. For example, my author page is set to a "public" setting, as the general

---

2 The celebrity in question wound up being held up at gunpoint, while being robbed of millions of dollars in property.

public needs to have ready access to that page. However, the page is also closely monitored, and if anyone behaves inappropriately (to me or to any member of the page), they are immediately blocked and reported to Facebook. Conversely, my personal page setting is for Facebook friends only, with the exception of any work-related appearances that I make (those specific posts are set to "public").

Once you have set your privacy settings, check regularly to make sure those settings remain where you want them. Glitches can and do happen, and, from time to time, policies and features change on the site.

2) **Remember that the Internet is *forever***: Understand that once something is posted to the Internet, it is in cyberspace forever. Yes, you can delete posts and pictures after posting them; however, as referenced above, people are also capable of "screengrabbing," which is basically taking a picture of a screen prior to deletion. Don't believe me? Just look at the number of political figures, celebrities, and public figures whose previous Facebook posts, Twitter posts, and Instagram pictures have come back to haunt them even after deletion, not to mention situations where people did not get jobs once their social media was "investigated."[3]

The beauty of posting on the Internet is that you have the opportunity to think twice (or more) before hitting *post* or *share*. Prior to posting, read your post carefully, and then read it again. Then read it one more time.

---

3 If you're interviewing for any position anywhere, a search of your social media presence is something that you *must* assume automatically takes place.

You've Got a "Friend"?

Since it is literally the largest social media platform in the world, let's spend a little time discussing Facebook and the specific issues surrounding the matter of "friending." Friend requests are generally fun to send and receive. What a great way to connect (or re-connect) with family, loved ones, and friends from our present and our past. I genuinely treasure the people with whom I grew up, went to school, worked, and/or knew socially, and I take great pleasure in being connected with them via social media. Beyond the friend factor, Facebook is also a great way to be socially, civically, and politically active within one's community, join different groups sharing common interests and hobbies, build or maintain a business, and in sum, be an active and vital part of the world.

As much fun as all of this may be, social media is also rife with fake accounts, scammers, and predators. To Facebook's credit specifically, they do make efforts to track and eliminate this particular element from their social network; however, it's really a game of whack-a-mole for them and for most social platforms: one fake account is deleted and two more pop up to take its place. For this reason, and regardless of how alone and lonely you might be feeling, you *must* exercise tremendous caution with *any* friend requests that you send and/or accept.

Check Them Out

Whether the request originates from a male or female, when receiving a friend request, my personal checklist is as follows:

1) Do I know this person (from work, from school, growing up, social activities, etc.)? If I don't personally know (or remember) them ...

2) Do I have any mutual friends in common and, if so, from what circle are those mutual friends?[4]

I then proceed to their profile to continue checking:

1) How long have they been on Facebook?
2) Do they have both a profile picture and a cover picture (the larger box on the page)?
3) What does their timeline posting tell you about them?

If I don't know someone personally and/or have mutual friends with them; if they have just joined Facebook and have no posts or cover pictures; if their timeline posting consists of nothing but a profile picture, I reject the friend request. If appropriate, I report the profile to Facebook as a possible fake account so that they may investigate the profile.

This may sound very time consuming; however, it takes longer to teach than to actually accomplish. It is worth a few quick steps to ensure that my page remains safe and that I and those connected to both of my pages remain secure.

Fakers and Scammers and Screwballs—Oh My!

It's Saturday night and you're all alone. Feeling bored, lonely, or perhaps a combination of the two (something to which we can all relate), you are meandering around Facebook, when you receive a

---

4 Note that Facebook will let you know if you have friends in common.

friend request. You click on it and are greeted by a profile photo of an attractive soldier in military uniform.[5] Their whereabouts are stated as being in a foreign country; their marital status states that they are widowed. Perhaps there are a few pictures of them in "action," maybe one or two with a young child. There is no cover photo; there's only a blank, black space and, other than those few pictures, they don't have a lot of posts—but hey, they're deployed and fighting a war or on a top-secret mission...how much time can they possibly have to mess around with social media?

You accept the friend request and almost immediately begin receiving messages from your new soldier friend. They are attractive, funny, charming, smart—all the things that have been missing in your life. You begin corresponding immediately and constantly. You yearn to see that message notification from them and when those notifications arrive, they say all the right things: you are the most beautiful woman/handsome man they've ever seen, they feel as though they can talk to you about anything, all of the things that we all love to hear. In no time, they declare their love for you. They can't wait to meet you, put their arms around you—they even start talking about planning a future with you.

Then they ask for money. It is an emergency involving their child, they are in a faraway land, they have no one else to whom they can turn, and they love you *so* much. Can you please help?

Do you get out your checkbook or hightail it to a place that will wire money? Or do you dare to allow yourself to think that perhaps this is all a scam? Because in all likelihood, it *is* a scam.

---

5 This can be either sex—men get scammed as well.

I wish I could tell you that the above scenario was born of my creativity and imagination. Sadly, I'm not a fiction writer; nor am I especially creative. This scenario is tragically common and, though both men and women have been and continue to be victimized by online scammers, statistics currently show that women are victimized slightly more often than men. I am reminded of the story of a widow who sought online friendship after the sudden death of her husband. She eventually "met" someone online who she honestly believed would be the next special man in her life. Several months, many lies, and a financial loss numbering in the hundreds of thousands later, she discovered that everything about him (including his name) was a scam.

I receive countless numbers of friend requests, most of which picture alleged members of the military as described earlier. The horrific part is that beyond the scam itself, the pictures are of real soldiers, pictures that have been "lifted" from legitimate social media accounts, dating websites, etc., and are used to create fake accounts that, in turn, are used to elicit money from vulnerable, grief-stricken, and largely unsuspecting victims. Remember that friend request checklist? There's a reason for it. Use it often and use it wisely.

Savvy Equals Safety

There are several other precautions that you'll want to take in using social media:

1) **Anyone who requests money of you through social media gets immediately blocked:** When I say "anyone" that means *anyone*. If the request for money appears to be coming from

someone you know, do *not* automatically trust the request, as your trusted friend and/or their profile account may have been hacked. Contact the person who appears to be asking for money via e-mail or phone to double-check that the message came from them—and keep *all* financial dealings off of social media and out of public view.

2) **Use caution in joining groups:** As you have already read, I'm an advocate for joining Facebook groups with whom you share commonalities, not the least of which is widowhood. You can meet wonderful new friends who understand exactly what it is that you are going through, whatever "it" happens to be at the moment. In addition to broadening your own widowhood/grief recovery community, there are many other groups encompassing all manner of hobbies, interests, faiths, political activities, and so much more than I could possibly list. In joining Facebook groups, you'll want to remember to:

   a. **Make sure that the group and/or the person for whom the page is named is legitimate in all respects:** You always want to make sure that a person is who they say they are and/or that the page or group that you are joining is who and what they represent themselves to be. These pages will have completed and thorough Facebook profiles, and will generally include at least one website address prominently displayed. This allows you to conduct additional confirmation that the group/person is who and what they say they are.

   b. **Beware of the numbers:** A brand-new or nearly new individual or group page with a disproportionate number of "likes" has most likely purchased those likes from what are known as *click farms*—generally offshore companies that sell likes in the form of fake accounts in order to falsely inflate a person's notoriety or a page's importance or influence. Check out when the page was established. Unless you are an A-list celebrity who has just joined social media, the chances that you going from zero to 50,000 likes in twelve hours is extremely low.

Those who have little to no presence in the media, are not on a regular speaking circuit, are not selling a popular product of some kind (think bestselling books or music), are not a sizeable organization, or are not otherwise exposed to large numbers of people on a regular basis, will not likely garner huge amounts of likes. Further, if someone is boasting more likes than actual celebrities, political figures, well-known and established authors, household names, etc., something is definitely amiss.

c. **Hold on to your money.** Don't get me wrong; many legitimate charities and non-profit 501(c)(3) organizations have a social media presence, as do politicians and others who are in the business of raising money to a noble end. However, legitimate groups will generally have a "donate" button on their page or other direction as to how you can financially contribute to their cause. If a group begins constantly badgering you for money or attempts to charge you to be a member of a social media page, it's a red flag.

Before you donate money (or anything else for that matter), make sure that you are donating to a reputable non-profit, easily checked through CharityWatch, GuideStar, and other watchdog groups. You can also go directly to a non-profit or fundraiser's website, all of which will generally have their 501(c)(3) non-profit information posted. Do your homework and your research to make sure that your money and/or other donations are going where they need to go.

3) **Make friends, meet people, have fun . . . but keep your savvy:** The Internet gives people a feeling of security because when you're using the Internet, you are usually within the safe surroundings of your home, and that feeling of security can transfer to online communication. However, you must remember that especially when it comes to meeting people through social media, you are initially communicating with strangers. You'd be shocked at the number of people who give out their private information on social media to people they don't personally know. So let's continue to keep you safe.

   a. **If someone you've just met through social media sends you a message asking to meet you that same day or night, the answer is *no*:** Be it opposite sex or same sex, this rule is non-negotiable. A first message or a first e-mail is supposed to an introduction, and remember— *you don't know them!* Let them know that you don't meet up with new people after one message but that you'd like to get to know them better (if, in fact, you wish to pursue further communication). If they're not happy with this answer, you have just discovered one of the reasons for the "block" button . . . and all social media platforms have them.

b. **If someone is pushing you to reveal your personal information too soon, it's a huge warning sign:** Please heed that warning sign. For example, a popular ruse is, "I don't like to type, so just give me your phone number." You don't like to type? Well, that's just too damn bad. It's the twenty-first century; get a keyboard, learn to type—and the answer is *still* no. If someone continues to pressure you or gets aggressive in any way, they get blocked.

c. **Anyone (whether you know them personally or not) who sends messages or puts posts on your wall[6] that you feel are inappropriate, too personal, or perhaps downright offensive also gets blocked.** Paying a heartfelt compliment is lovely; however, things like questions about your finances, overtly sexual comments, or anything that you consider to be incendiary in nature are completely inappropriate.

d. **Beware the dreaded "catfish":** Let's say you have met someone through social media in whom you might be romantically interested, perhaps in one of your groups or through a legitimate friend request. You've messaged, e-mailed, texted, and talked on the phone. Things seem to be heading in the right direction, and this seems to be a really great person . . . but for some reason, they can never seem to find time to actually meet in person, or they constantly schedule and cancel dates. Meanwhile, the online and texting and telephone "relationship"

6 You can control who can post on your wall in your settings, which is a really good idea. If someone does attempt to post on your wall, it will be archived for your review, and you make the decision as to whether or not the post can go onto your wall.

continues full speed ahead. Let's say that this relationship even escalates to declarations of love. ***Beware: This is a huge, glow-in-the-dark, bright red flag!***

A television program entitled, *Catfish: The TV Show* features people who have been duped by online personas into believing that they were in a real relationship. It absolutely amazes me that these genuinely innocent, put-upon souls are on television, crying about how they were deceived and fooled and embarrassed and humiliated, and that may certainly be true. However, when they are asked how long their "relationship" has endured without having ever actually met the person with whom they were/are in love, these people sorrowfully reply with a figure that generally ends in the word *years*. Years? You've been communicating with someone for years, you declare that you are in love with them ... and you've never actually *met* them?

If someone whom you've never once met in person is declaring undying love and devotion to and for you, and this doesn't set off warning bells in your head, I honestly do not know what will. *Please* do not be so taken in by the fantasy of a new relationship that you lose all sight of reality. Messaging, texting, and telephones are supposed to be a precursor to meeting someone and then a subsequent way of continuing an in-person relationship. If a person appears to want to be in love only online or on the phone or in e-mail or a combination of all three, something is really, really *wrong*. Get away as fast as you can!

In sharing these stories and scenarios, do's and don'ts, the intent is not to frighten you away from social media and off of your computer. On the contrary, my goal is to continually inform and equip you with the information that you need to keep yourself safe and secure. My hope is that you will safely and freely enjoy all of the wonderful aspects of social media, truly a forum that can be not only a valuable tool in your healing journey arsenal, but one that can also be the gateway to wonderful new friendships and experiences.

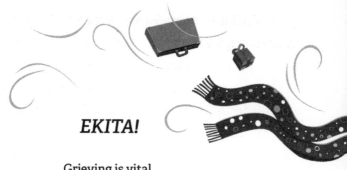

EKITA!

Grieving is vital.
It's an essential process,
regardless of what anyone may say, believe, or tell you.

❤

No one who has been widowed will ever say,
"Don't be sad."
No one who has been widowed will ever say,
"Don't miss your beloved."
No one who has been widowed will ever say,
"Quit grieving."
No one who has been widowed will ever say,
"It's time for you to be over it."

❤

Nobody expects you to be grieving one day and happy the next,
for grief recovery doesn't happen easily or quickly.
There is no such thing as "instant happy" after loss.
There's no such thing as "loss today, live it up tomorrow."
There's no such thing as avoiding the inevitable path to healing.
There can be no true healing without first processing grief
and paying it the honor and time that it warrants and deserves.

❤

However,
if you remain in a place of sorrow,

if grief becomes the nucleus of your existence,
you can't eventually flourish . . .
which is what you deserve to do.

❤

Sorrow cannot become your core,
the place inside you from where you operate
and the very essence of who and what is you.
You cannot thrive while remaining in a place of sorrow.
You cannot focus solely on sorrow,
nor can you permit yourself to be around those who
would encourage you to
keep sorrow as your focus.
Get around that which is and those who are going to lift you
and help you move forward.

❤

Healing is indeed a process.
It's all about learning to thrive
rather than simply survive.
Be patient with your process.

❤

You are learning.
You are growing.
You are healing.
And while it may be neither fast nor easy,
you *will* get there.

❤

Most of all, remember that you deserve better than
sorrow acting as your core
. . . and you know it.

Bereavement
Boot Camp Lesson Seven:
It's *Your* Turn

Welcome to Boot Camp Lesson Seven, a "companion" to your sixth lesson. Let's start with a really big word: *initiative*. Why is initiative such a huge word? Because initiative means taking action instead of merely reacting. Initiative takes intent. Initiative takes formulation. Initiative takes follow-up and follow through. Initiative comes from within yourself.

Initiative is also likely the last thing on your mind when you're dealing with loss, and I completely get that. After Mike died, I didn't have much initiative (or energy) for anything other than brushing my teeth—and on some days, I'm not sure I even accomplished that task much before 6:00 PM. We all have our "have-to's," of course, going to work, taking care of a household, and so forth. I suppose that the initiative for those activities is innate and easily explained—we like to eat, have roofs over our collective heads, and the ability to pay the bills. However, what about taking initiative in other areas of our lives that are not included on a have-to list?

Many who are in the midst of grief recovery complain that their phone is not ringing off the hook with invitations to go out, stay in, or get together. They feel forgotten, they feel isolated, and worst of all, of course, they feel horribly lonely. My question to those who complain is, "How many telephone calls have *you* made? How many invitations have *you* extended?" I am then generally met with a startled look, as if to say, "You mean *I* should pick up a telephone?" accompanied by a response to the effect of, "Why should I be the one who has to make a call/issue an invitation/ instigate a get-together/make the first move? After all, I'm the one who is suffering."

There is no argument: you are indeed the one who is suffering. However, there is one major problem with that attitude. While you're certainly justified in your feelings, the reality is that many people (including those who know and love you) are not always quick to reach out for the simple reason that they're not quite sure what to do with or about you right now. They're afraid of saying the "wrong thing"—so they say nothing. They're afraid of doing the "wrong thing"—so they do nothing. They're afraid of calling too early in the day, and they are afraid of calling too late in the evening. They are afraid of calling too soon after your loss, and they're afraid of what you'll think if time has passed without a phone call, generally unaware that allowing even *more* time to pass is not the solution. They are afraid of disturbing you. They are afraid that if they mention your loss, you'll spontaneously combust (or a reaction similar thereto). Yet they know your loss event to be the proverbial elephant in the room.

In short, they're afraid. *Of you.*

I spend a lot of time educating the world on how to handle loss and challenge, and how to best help someone who may be going through a life-altering situation. However, until the world collectively gets the message, the reality is that it will occasionally be up to *you* to put the people around you at ease. This is where the word *initiative* comes in. Even though, in principle, you shouldn't have to worry about putting others at ease during a time of loss, the fact remains that it may be up to you to do just that. Someone you know may be aching to spend time with you but is allowing their fear to stop them from making that call or sending that e-mail. Meanwhile, you are on the other end of these relationships, staring at a silent phone or at an empty e-mail inbox and thinking that everyone has "forgotten" about that through which you are suffering… and that no one truly cares.

So, while initiative is indeed a huge word, it is also something that you need to put into practice. Instead of waiting for the phone to ring, it's time for *you* to take initiative. Quit waiting around for everyone else to do the inviting. Let people know that while you've been knocked down, you have no intention of staying down. Let those in your inner circle know that you'd like to spend a little time with them in whatever pursuit(s) would be comfortable for you. It can be anything from a quiet lunch to a few sets of tennis.

Who is it in your life right now with whom you would like to spend a little time?[1] Who would serve as the best kind of company

---

1 Here's a helpful hint: Make absolutely positive that they're one of your Energy Givers.

for you? Who haven't you heard from that you know with absolute certainty is concerned about you all the same? Why not get that person or those people onto your calendar and back into your life right now?

Initiative. Take it.
Reach out. Stop waiting and start doing. Pick up the telephone. Send the e-mail.
Make the plans.

It's *your* turn now.
Here's your seventh Boot Camp Affirmation. Keep it with you:

I recognize that even during times of loss, relationships are still a two-way street. As I continue my proactivity on my healing journey, I will initiate invitations with those in my life who represent support and positivity. I will no longer wait for others to do the inviting all of the time. I also understand that people may be hesitating to call or invite me out because they're afraid of intruding, and I'll reassure those people that I'm receptive to their calls and invitations.

Boot Camp Challenge

Contact just *one* person this week and invite them to do something that fits into your current comfort zone. As with your previous Boot Camp Challenge, it can be quietly social (a movie, dinner, or lunch) or, if you're feeling ready, you might consider having a few friends over to your house for drinks and appetizers or coffee and dessert. Whatever you feel comfortable doing is fine. It all begins with just one phone call or e-mail that originates with *you*.

Within the next week, I'm going to contact _____

_____

_____

_____

_____

And invite them to _____

_____

_____

_____

_____

How I felt after we got together _____

_____

_____

_____

_____

_____

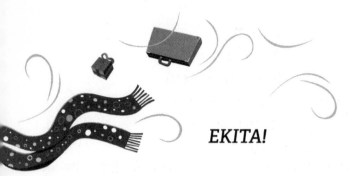

EKITA!

Death may knock you down.
Grief may knock you down.
Life challenges may knock you down.
People may try to knock you down.
However, no matter the circumstances,
you don't have to *stay* down.

♥

Get back up.
It may be more difficult this time.
It may take longer to find your feet.
But you've done it before . . . perhaps many times.
And you can do it again now.

♥

You got back up
the day after your beloved
left your embrace.
You got back up
the day after the funeral.
You got back up
when it was time to go back to work.
You can do it again now.

❤

You got back up
after the first time someone
questioned your judgment or your healing journey
(perhaps more than once).
You got back up
when it felt like those on whom you once counted
chose instead to willingly leave your life.
You got back up
when you thought all hope was lost.
And you can do it again now.

❤

You got back up
so that you could learn how to live again.
You got back up
because you knew that your children were watching
and learning from your path and your choices.
You got back up
to help your children learn the same lessons.
And you can do it again now.

❤

No matter what life circumstances knock you down,
no matter who tries to knock you down,
get back up.
You've gotten back up before
and you *can* do it again now.

It's a Matter of Life...
and Debt: Know Your Rights

I t was scarcely one month after Mike's death, when I awakened one morning to an envelope sent by a dauntingly large and intimidating law firm; something that no one needs to receive immediately after you have buried your beloved. Left in both emotional and financial ruin at that point, I was also recovering from major emergency abdominal surgery, and my father had just been diagnosed with the terminal liver cancer that took his life shortly thereafter. It was not an especially great season in time.

I anxiously tore open the envelope and was floored at its contents. After a terse and incredibly disingenuous, "Sorry for your loss" salutation, the letter went on to state that the Law Firm of Dauntingly Large and Intimidating were representing a financial institution that held a credit card and a credit line belonging to Mike, both opened seven years prior to our marriage. The letter further stated that I was "obviously responsible" for "taking care of your husband's obligations," and that if they didn't receive full and final payment on both the credit card and credit line within thirty days, they would initiate further action against me. This is in spite of the fact that, while I held my own credit card, credit line, and both my business and personal accounts at the same institution, my name had never been associated on the particular accounts that Mike held, nor had I ever once utilized these (or any of his) accounts.

Oh yeah ... did I forget to mention that despite Mike's more than twenty-five year history with them, the actual financial institution never once contacted me personally, instead simply referring the matter to a law firm? Did I also neglect to mention that almost all of the officers and many of the employees of said financial institution were guests at our wedding? *And* at his funeral? Do I have to tell you how *enraged* I was?

Rather than contact me personally, the matter was instead hastily referred to a law firm, ostensibly with the ultimate goals of (a) taking advantage of a grieving and vulnerable widow, and (b) intimidating said widow into forking over a quick buck. Moreover, they were clearly attempting to collect on debts for which they knew (and more to the point, *I* knew) that I was not legally responsible. So, despite the rage, the vulnerability, and an extremely sore abdomen, I dusted off my own legal prowess[1] and sent them a letter in response. I none-too-kindly informed them that Mike's accounts and the debts associated with them were not in my name, that any debt owing was amassed long before we were married, and if they continued to

---

[1] By education and degree, I'm a certified paralegal and settlement negotiator. I'm also fluent in the language of legalese. Therefore, I'm not averse to periodically "stretching" my legal legs when unfairly challenged.

harass me, they too would be hearing from an extremely large and intimidating law firm. I never heard from them again.

It thereafter took me about a half hour to pay off and close my credit card, pay off and close the credit line, and move every cent in my accounts to another financial institution, which was only too happy to welcome both myself and my finances.

Know Your Rights

When you are in the throes of grief, matters of finance and legality are the last things with which you want to be concerned. However, and sadly, there are those who are only too happy to take advantage of both your emotional state, as well as what may be a lack of knowledge as to your rights as a widowed survivor. Even though it's absolutely the last thing you want to think about, when it comes to debt after death, you *must* know your rights, regardless of whether or not you are personally responsible for the debt:

1) **Depending on certain factors, you may not be responsible for debts left behind by your spouse or loved one.** If the debts do not have your name on them, you may not be liable for the debt incurred. However, as with all other financial and legal matters, laws as to financial liability after spousal death vary widely from state to state as well as from country to country. Generally speaking, you will be responsible for any debt to which your name is attached in any way (whether you are co-owner of an asset or an authorized user on a credit card). However, you must consult with an attorney who specializes in estate matters and/or a CPA to determine your actual financial responsibility. Do not make assumptions on your own.

2) **No matter who is accountable for remaining debt, *no one*
    has the right to employ abusive, threatening, or harassing
    tactics in order to collect.** The Federal Trade Commission
    is responsible for enforcing the Fair Debt Collection Prac-
    tices Act.[2] This means that if you live anywhere in the United
    States, you're protected against illegal collection tactics.
    Unfortunately, this doesn't mean that some collectors don't
    attempt to employ these tactics, especially with those who
    may be vulnerable (like the naïve and/or the grieving), any-
    one who might be easily frightened or intimidated (such as
    those in their late teens or twenties, the elderly, or those who
    are new to the United States), or those who simply are not
    fully aware of their rights. There are a variety of protections
    in place to safeguard against these predators, and in extreme
    cases, these protections may also help you sue for damages
    against any company or organization that violates state or
    federal collection laws.

When it comes to settling debts left behind in the wake of spousal death, you *must* know your rights. You can't permit yourself to
be intimidated or be otherwise so overwhelmed with grief, exhaus-
tion, confusion, or a combination of all three, that you take the
path of least resistance (or greatest fear) and simply start doling
out money.

Finally, you must be willing to advocate for yourself (or find
experts who will advocate on your behalf) and *demand* to be
treated with respect, with dignity, and within the limits of the law.
Accept nothing less—from anyone.

---

2 For more information, visit *www.consumer.ftc.gov*.

EKITA!

Why should members of the widowed community
be referred to as "heroes"?
Because they are indeed . . . heroes.

♥

The widowed will not necessarily accept
the word *hero* graciously,
instead believing the word to be self-serving or
arrogant when used in reference to them.
They will use different words.
They will brush the term aside.
They will self-deprecate,
seeing nothing special or extraordinary in the person who is
looking back at them in the mirror.
Nevertheless, heroes they are.

♥

The widowed are handed a set of horrific circumstances
that no one deserves.
Their families are torn apart,
first by death and then often by discord
that can eventually leave the widowed to fend alone.
Many endure financial and emotional hardships

that those outside the widowed community
cannot and would not wish to fathom.

❤

With little time to pay to their grief, the widowed are expected to
carry on every single day with heads held high,
even though their hearts are broken and silently weeping.
They return to work, raise children, and run households,
even though they're not sure how they themselves
are going to go on.
Many don't have the support system that
they both need and deserve.

❤

And yet . . . they persevere.
The widowed persevere with a steely resolve and determination
that few understand or appreciate.
They seek support and education because they realize that
they're entitled to better than what life has handed to them.
Filled with hope, they courageously face their respective todays
while dreaming of brighter tomorrows
and are willing to do what it takes to fulfill those dreams.

❤

Being willing to do what it takes:
this is the very definition of hero—
and the widowed community boasts heroes in abundance.

Loyalty Versus Living Again: Are *You* Being "Disloyal"?

Let's face it. Telling someone how to grieve after a loss is rather like trying to tell someone how to raise their children —it's generally unwelcome advice to which no one listens anyway. So even after many years, four books, countless appearances, and hundreds of thousands of letters, I *still* never tell anyone how to grieve. I give advice only when asked and even then, my guidance usually falls into one of two unspoken and informal categories:

(a) ***"This worked really well for me."***

or

(b) ***"PLEASE don't make the same mistake(s) that I made."***

You have likely ascertained by the tenor of this book that my approach to grief recovery has always been slightly different than more mainstream, garden-variety approaches, and I happily embrace that difference. I further recognize that when you take a somewhat unconventional approach to a subject as sensitive as loss, not everyone is going to get what you are doing or how you choose to do it. I also understand (and obviously teach) that there are a wide variety of ways to facilitate grief recovery and that those dealing with grief of any kind must seek out and avail themselves of whatever tools will best speak to them, touch their hearts, motivate their minds, inspire and inform their actions, and ultimately best serve their respective healing journeys.

But what happens when those who I am sure have good intentions approach those in your community with a point of view that is polar opposite to what you believe and have been teaching for years?

Moreover, what if that point of view is potentially dangerous to the emotionally fragile?

Talk about a conundrum.

A few years ago, I was made aware of a group promoting their particular version of "grief recovery" and whose mission statement included philosophies that fly in the face of everything that I firmly believe and continue to teach. If interpreted correctly, this group stated that they are "loyally" widowed; apparently defined as those who consider themselves still married to someone who is no longer physically here. Conversely, I have always taught that after the loss of a spouse, eventually continuing forward with life in *all* respects is not only okay, it is a right that is earned just by being on earth. I also staunchly believe and maintain that seeking companionship, falling in love again, and/or remarrying does not equal disloyalty or "cheating" (about which you will learn more later in the book)—and that while you can, should, and will always love your late spouse, the heart expands infinitely to welcome new love and a new life if you choose it.

I truly do live by the words from your earlier EKITA:

"You can honor your past,
you can treasure your past,
you can love your past . . .
you do not have to LIVE in your past"

You can see the dilemma.

Upon learning of this particular group, I shot right past being annoyed and went straight to feeling horribly hurt; for my late husband, for the life that we built and led together, for the implications being made, and for the people whom I serve, all of whom were now being handed one whale of a mixed and potentially damaging message.

Remember what I said at the beginning of the chapter—I do not tell others how to grieve or how to find their peace during the most devastating time in their lives . . . and I never will. However, I also will not remain quiet while others disrespectfully question a widowed's love for or loyalty to a late spouse simply because a choice was correctly made to move forward into a new life.

To my mind, "loyalty" to a late spouse means keeping their legacies alive. For me, loyalty to Mike and to his memory meant continuing his legacies of love and service to the community. Loyalty meant raising a daughter to adulthood in a way that would have made her daddy proud. Loyalty meant fulfilling Mike's dying requests to "*Go find love again*" and "*Use our experience to help others.*" Loyalty means living an abundant life and teaching others how to do the same. In other words, ALS had already claimed Mike's life, and I was not about to let it claim my life and the lives of our family as well. I was determined to design and live a new life and teach my daughter to do the same . . . and we both eventually accomplished that bold goal.

Is this then considered "disloyalty"?

I am not a theologian; however, to the best of my knowledge and regardless of faith, the words in most wedding ceremonies are by and large the same:

"Until death do us part."

Even religions in which one marries for "time and eternity" permit the widowed to remarry for their remaining time spent on earth. Furthermore, all religions teach, choose, and encourage *life* and living that life to its fullest.

Now, it is important to understand that there is absolutely *nothing* wrong with choosing to remain on your own post-loss, if indeed that is your *choice*. However, remaining alone because of ill-perceived or imagined disloyalty (and the resulting guilt) is just plain wrong.

Let there be no question in your mind that along with myself, most who have been widowed are now and will always be loyal to the love and memory of their late spouses. That will never change.

However, I do not buy into the statements that I heard at a support group many years ago, where people were saying things like, *"I'm just waiting until it's my time to go,"* or, *"I guess I'll be with him/her soon."* Is this *really* what our late spouses wanted for us?[1]

We are all entitled to everything and anything that life has to offer, and we should not have our love or loyalty for late spouses (or our children's love for and loyalty to their absent parent) questioned because we made a choice to grieve, recover, lovingly remember, and live *forward*.

I have *chosen* the life that I lead today, full of its trials and tribulations, triumphs and celebrations, and I teach my daughters (both biological and "bonus") to do the same. I have *chosen* to fully and completely love and embrace my new life, while remaining steadfast in my love for Mike and the memory of the life that we built and shared until he drew his final breath. I have *chosen* a life in service to others, which, in my opinion, is the best life that one can lead.

I have indeed chosen *life* . . . and I strongly encourage you and anyone who has been touched by the pain of loss to do the same.

Doing so does not now, nor will it *ever*, make you "disloyal" . . . to anyone.

Doing so simply makes you alive.

---

1 I encourage you to pay especially close attention to the EKITA immediately following this chapter.

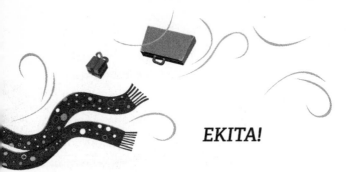

EKITA!

People often share what they believe that your late beloved
"wants" and does not "want" for you,
perhaps momentarily forgetting that no one
knew them better than you.
Keeping in mind that most of these people
also want you to heal
and are trying to provide comfort to you,
please also ponder the following . . .

♥

Imagine for a moment that your situation is reversed.
You were the one who crossed over and
left your spouse and your loved ones behind.
What would you want for THEM?
What kind of future would you want THEM to pursue?
What do you envision for THEM?

♥

Chances are excellent that whatever you wish for your spouse
is what they would want for YOU as well.
Keep this personal vision in your mind as you continue
forward on your healing journey.
It helps.

Comparing
Yourself to Others:
Why You Need to Stop

Comparisons. We all make them. I'm not talking about comparing ourselves to the impossibly perfect images that we see in print or on screen[1] but, rather, the comparisons that we tend to make in our everyday lives.

᠁

Meet my friend Lee. I believe that Lee has discovered the secret of the forty-one-hour day and is holding out on the rest of us. Blessed with four children and a globetrotting husband, she too travels the country for her own career, yet she always has time for everything and everyone. She is an active participant in her children's busy lives and runs a bustling household. She bakes and

---

1 Even though—and let's be honest—we sometimes do that too.

blogs; parents and presides over a charitable foundation; always looks amazing, and she never *ever* fails to return an e-mail from wherever she is on the planet—at all times of the day and night. Oh, and did I mention that she is also a renowned, bestselling author in her own right?

(As an aside, I have one-half of the number of children that she has, and those children are adults. I can't remember the last time I baked, but I'm positive that there was either bribery or a holiday involved, and my e-mail return rate is usually within the same *month* that I receive them).[2]

Do I find myself making comparisons to Lee? Of course I do, laughing all the while. This comparison is hilarious and harmless, a fun contrast mixed in with admiration for Lee's talents and, most importantly, her generous heart and spirit. However, there is another kind of comparison occurring far too often within the widowed community, and these comparisons are no laughing matter. In fact and unfortunately, these comparisons can actually be hurtful. Over and over again, too many in the widowed community ask: "Why can't I be more like 'them'?"

A widowed meets others through social media or in a support group who have done something just a bit sooner on their healing journeys. Perhaps it is the widow who has gone out on her first date or gotten a new job after years away from the workplace. Maybe it's the widower who courageously made a big change: sold a home or pursued a dream career or hobby. Whatever the case, a great many

---

2 Just for the record, I make the world's greatest taco salad, and I can draw a straight line with liquid eyeliner. Don't laugh—it's a start.

widowed are looking at others who might be just a little further along in their recovery, and the lament echoes:

"Why can't I be more like 'them'?"

You know why you can't be more like "them"? Because you are *you*! We are each unique individuals. Even if we lost our spouses in the exact same fashion, our journeys prior to and since losing our spouses are singular. You must embrace *your* particular journey, as well as keep control of the healing journey that belongs to you alone.

I know of widowed who begin dating within a few months after their losses. Others have waited for years to do so. There are widowed who happily remarry and others who choose to remain contentedly on their own. Some sell their homes immediately and others never leave the homes that they shared with their late spouses. There are widowed who back off on their careers and those who launch their careers into high gear. Some make huge careers changes or retire from the workplace altogether, in order to volunteer or travel the world. The one common denominator is that every single widowed out there is making the choices that are right for them and for their own healing journeys.

Now, if you are not where you'd like to be in your journey, if you feel as though you'd like to be further along and just don't know how to move forward, that's another story, and there is an abundance of help and support available (including right here). However, don't compare your journey to any other widowed or to others who have lost loved ones. Your journey is not a competition and it's not a race to some imaginary finish line.

Remember that when we compare ourselves to others, we rarely draw a true parallel. Instead, we inevitably compare our weaknesses (real or imagined) with others' strengths; a self-sabotaging and self-defeating exercise. Others are on *their* healing journeys. You need to be on and respect *your* healing journey and *your* processes.

Rather than pay too much attention to what everyone else is doing (and when or how they are doing it), pay attention to *you*. Pay attention to how *you* want your journey to unfold and what *your* future holds. Take pride in what you've accomplished, no matter how large or small, and you know what? I'll bet that there is at least one widowed out there who would marvel at how far *you* have come.

Others are doing things in their own way and in their own time. You deserve the same privilege.

EKITA!

Sometimes it's easier to just stay where we are.

To keep still.

Stay put.

Be quiet.

Suffer in silence.

❤

Sometimes it's just too hard to even try to move

away from pain

away from misery

away from fear

away from doubt.

❤

Sometimes it's easier to just stay where we are

than it is to do what it takes to move forward.

Despite how miserable we may feel by staying in a place of pain

a place of misery

a place of fear

a place of doubting

that life will ever again be good.

❤

The reality?

We'll remain the same

until the pain of remaining the same becomes greater
than the pain of change.
Change can indeed be painful.
But to move forward from the pain, the misery,
the fear, and the doubt . . .
change you must.

❤

How does change happen?
It begins with believing that embracing life again
is not only okay for you to do,
it is, in fact, the *right* thing to do.

❤

So beginning today.
Believe.
Begin to embrace life with all your heart.
Take one tiny step in the forward-focused direction
of your choosing.
Just one.

❤

Sometimes it's easier to just stay where you are,
until you take one tiny step forward—
away from pain
away from misery
away from fear
away from doubt.
And toward the discovery that
staying in a place of misery is no longer an option.

❤

Take one step forward.
You can do this.

28

Bereavement Boot Camp Lesson Eight: Past, Present, and Future— You *Can* Have All Three

Welcome to your last Bereavement Boot Camp lesson. I hope that your Boot Camp lessons have been a positive period of growth, discovery, and perhaps just a little bit of anticipation for the future. As we wrap up, I want to share a brief story that I hope you will take to heart and incorporate into your healing journey: remembering your past, embracing your today, and looking to your future.

I had been widowed for just over a year when my mother gave me very wise advice that I follow to this very day. At that moment in time and in addition to Mike's passing, I had also endured a year that included the suicide death of my uncle ten days prior to Mike's death, major emergency abdominal surgery three weeks after Mike's death, and the death of my father shortly after losing Mike.[1]

It was at that moment in time that Mom told me to stop and look back at how far I had progressed—and that's exactly what I did. In terms of a healing journey, one year (especially the first year) doesn't seem very long, and with good reason: it really *isn't* very long. However, when I actually stopped and examined how far I'd progressed up to that point (and how far I have progressed since that time), I began to truly appreciate the healing that I had accomplished. To this very day, I still take those occasional pauses to look back and remind myself just how far I have traveled since that awful season in time, when I thought that I would never see light or know love ever again.

In that same spirit, I invite you to take a periodic pause to stop, look back, and see just how far you've come—whether your loss was ten months ago, ten years ago, or ten days ago. In fact, why not pause right now and examine how far you've come since you began reading this book?

As you continue forward on your healing journey, be reminded to do the following:

1) **Continually make the conscious choice to keep healing and moving into your future:** It seems rather obvious, but believe it or not, many people do not make a mindful choice to begin (or continue) the healing process. Remember that just by being here, we're entitled to every abundance, happiness, and dream that we want to chase—but you have to *choose* to do so.

---

1 It was also a year that included September 11, 2001.

2) **Make time to grieve in the ways that *you* see fit:** Most of us don't have the luxury of giving in to our grief whenever the spirit takes us. We're at work, we're driving the kids, we're running errands … we're usually running *somewhere*.[2] However, you must remember that if you do not take the time to grieve, your grief will come back to bite you at some point—this is an absolute guarantee. By setting aside "me" time (with no distractions), you allow yourself to move through the grieving process in a healthy way.

3) **Always choose *proactive* coping versus *reactive* coping:** We generally can't control loss situations, but we do have control over our *reactions* to how things are going to unfold moving forward. Continue your proactivity by enriching yourself with education and community. Reading this book and putting the Boot Camp lessons into practice is a great start, but you need to continue your education beyond this book, and become (or remain) an active part of a healing community.

4) **Take conscious ownership of your healing journey:** Actually own your journey. I mean really *own* it. It belongs to *you*. After you assume (and believe in) ownership, you'll subconsciously and automatically emanate and convey this message to the people around you. Let everyone know exactly who's in charge and *mean* it. As long as you are not coping in a destructive manner, as long as you are meeting your responsibilities and obligations, and as long as you're not hurting yourself or anyone around you, however you choose to design and proceed is entirely up to *you*.

---

2 And if you are anything like me, you are usually running about fifteen minutes behind.

5) **Don't be afraid to keep the memories alive:** You absolutely can keep memories alive and part of your present without remaining in a place of sorrow. Encourage school-age children to display pictures in their bedrooms and school lockers. Enjoy reminiscing through family photos and videos. Remember loved ones on birthdays, anniversaries, and holidays in creative ways. If the tears come, let them come; that's perfectly okay too.

6) **Reach out for help:** No one—myself included—can help anyone begin a healing journey "sooner," but as long as you reach out, you can begin receiving help right now.

If you haven't been able to complete every single challenge throughout the Boot Camp process, it really *is* okay. If you weren't quite ready to take on any one of the challenges, it simply means that you weren't ready at that particular moment in time. Who knows where you will be in your healing journey process next week or next month? This is the beauty of owning a book. If you weren't or aren't ready for any one (or all) of the challenges when you initially read them, you can always revisit those challenges any time that you wish and try again. And again. And yet again.

Here's your eighth and final Boot Camp Affirmation:

I embrace that I can't control the fact that I have suffered a huge loss. However, I *can* control my reactions to my loss, as well as what I am going to do with the life that I have been handed. Whatever I decide to do and whatever direction that I decide to take, I will do so with the understanding that by exploring new opportunities and experiences, I am not casting aspersion upon or disrespecting my past. I'm actually taking control of a situation over which I have had little or no control by honoring my past without living in my past, welcoming each new day and designing both my future and my destiny.

Final Boot Camp Challenge

The best way to measure your progression is to see it in action. Stop for just a moment and think back over the entire time since your loss (the length of time that has elapsed since your loss is immaterial). In the space below, jot down the way(s) that you've progressed on your journey. No progression is too small or insignificant. As you continue your journey, revisit this space and add items to your progress. You can also add the area(s) in which you feel you need additional help or where you'd like to make personal improvements. Don't forget to periodically revisit this space (every six months is a great barometer) and re-read your entries. You'll actually be able to see your own forward movement.

Positive progression on my healing journey includes:

_____

_____

_____

_____

_____

Areas where I feel I might need additional help or focus include:

_____

_____

_____

_____

Six-month checkup positive progression on my healing journey includes:

_____

_____

_____

_____

_____

Areas where I feel I might need additional help or focus include:

_____

_____

_____

_____

_____

One-year checkup positive progression on my healing journey includes:

_____

_____

_____

_____

_____

Areas where I feel I might need additional help or focus include:

_____

_____

_____

_____

_____

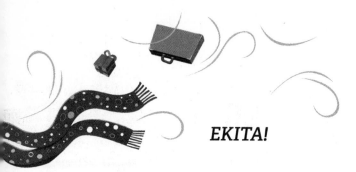

EKITA!

Healing comes with proactivity.

Healing comes with getting serious about getting better.

Healing comes in the doing,

the actions taken,

your new life blueprint being put into practice.

Be it widowhood or any other challenge or loss that you may face,

you *must* become and remain proactive with your healing.

Being here is a great beginning—

be sure to keep going.

When Family
and Friends "Forget":
Six Essential Tips

A s defined in Webster's Dictionary, widowhood is characterized as: "One who is made to be widowed by or through the loss of a spouse and who has not remarried."

However, in what is known as Widowed World, widowhood is defined as:

"A 'club' that absolutely no one willingly joins; a state of existence that will upend your entire life as you once knew it and forever transform the rest of your life from what you had previously and carefully designed, into a scary and uncertain future."

One of the most common complaints that I receive from the widowed is echoed in the following comments:

"Since my husband died, all of our friends have forgotten him
    and disappeared,"

"I haven't changed, but everyone around me is treating me dif-
    ferently. And that doesn't count the people who just left my
    life without a word."

"I guess I'm not allowed to talk about my wife anymore. No one
    else wants to, that's for sure. But she's still in my heart and
    no one understands that or even cares."

Reality check: While people really haven't forgotten your beloved,
it's going to be much easier for everyone else to move forward than
it will be for you. The fact is that *no one else* is going to be affected
by the loss of your spouse in the same profound ways that you are,
for one obvious reason: they are not the widowed. Absolutely no
one is going to feel this loss in the same ways that you do, because of
a differing loss perspective. You have also learned the unfortunate
fact that people are generally uncomfortable with the topic of loss
and honestly don't know what to do either with you or for you.

As you learned in Chapter Eleven ("Don't Speak . . ."), it is a sad
reality that some of the people whom you once believed to be dear
friends or family might choose to leave your life for myriad reasons. Part of transitioning into a life post-loss includes dealing with
relationships that may be in flux, evolving, or even disappearing
altogether. Following are six important tips on how to handle these
changes to facilitate your ultimate healing.

1. **Respect the different loss perspectives:** Your true friends
    and family will never disappear; however, they *will* move for-
    ward with their lives and be able to do so much sooner than
    you. Respect that their healing processes are much different

from yours. Just as no one can reasonably expect you to rapidly recover from the loss of your beloved, you cannot expect others to grieve in the same ways that you do.

2. **Get proactive:** Understand that during this difficult time, people will want to give you space and time to begin healing, or perhaps allow you some well-deserved rest. These same people are not going to want to bother you with daily phone calls or visits, instead leaving it to you to contact them. As outlined in Boot Camp Lesson Seven, take the initiative. If you're ready for quiet socializing, pick up the phone and let others know that you wouldn't mind a bit of company.

3. **Fear not:** Many will be afraid to bring up the subject of your loss for fear of upsetting you, when, of course, the exact opposite is true; *not* bringing up your loss actually feeds that damn elephant hanging out in the middle of the room. In point of fact, *you* may be the one who needs to put others at ease. If you want to talk about your late spouse, go ahead and talk about them! People will take their cues from you, and if *you* are fine with talking about your beloved, others will be comfortable talking about them as well. Share a wonderful memory. Tell a funny story. Most of all, don't *ever* be reluctant or afraid to talk about your beloved or otherwise worry about making others uncomfortable in doing so. If others can't handle it for whatever reason, they are the ones with the problem—not you.

4. **Embrace who you have become:** You are now beginning to understand that even though you obviously still feel like "you" on the inside, the fact is that you *have* changed. Remember that it is impossible to remain the same person

you were prior to widowhood; the experience changes you forever. However, while the circumstances are undeniably tragic, most do not ever get to discover the true depths of their strength, their mettle, and the tenacity that it takes to recover from what may be the most tragic experience of their lives. You not only have that knowledge, you should take pride and comfort in that knowledge.

5. **Learn to let go:** It is incredibly difficult to let go of friendships and relationships on which you may have once heavily depended. However, if people consciously choose not to be a supportive part of your healing journey, let go you must. You have dealt with enough negativity in your life just by the nature of what major loss brings. If those around you are not able or willing to be part of your healing process in a positive way, they do not get the privilege of being a part of your process—or your life—at all.

6. **Watch your "reach":** When seeking help and support, each of us has three distinct directions of reach: reaching down, reaching out, and reaching up. What are the differences?

   a. **Reaching down:** A lot of people reach down without even realizing it, because they are choosing the wrong people with whom they share their healing journey. Reaching down means that you're involving an Energy Drainer, and nothing positive can ever come of that. Don't ever reach down—for any reason.

   b. **Reaching out:** Reaching *out* is a good thing. I strongly encourage you to reach out *for* and *to* others in our community; your peers who are where you are and to share thoughts, feelings, and experiences. This is how you discover that whatever your experience, you are truly not alone. If nothing else, you'll be buoyed by the comfort of others who are exactly like you.

c. **Reaching up:** When it comes to seeking help and guidance, always reach *up*. Reach *up* to those who have gone before you; they are the people who will listen to your stories, your challenges, your fears, your goals, and your hopes with open hearts and enriched minds. Reach *up* to those who will celebrate the triumphs on your healing journey, no matter how incredibly big or seemingly small—because they have been before where you are now, and they will understand the significance of those triumphs. Reach *up* to experts; those whom you can trust to give you wise advice, counsel, ideas and suggestions on how to make your journey as peaceful as possible.

Because those of us who either are or ever have been a part of Widowed World in any way not only understand . . . we will *never* disappear.

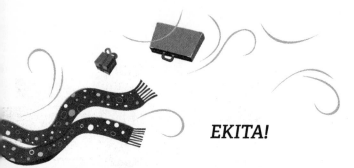

EKITA!

No one chose widowhood as a path in their lives.

No one chooses any of the unpleasant things that can also happen
as a result of the path that we were set upon.

You may have had no choice in being set upon this path.

However, you *do* have a choice in how your life can be going forward.

❤

You have a choice in how you are going to face every day.

You have a choice in how you're going to live the rest of your life.

You have a choice with your attitude,

the one with which you welcome the day,

and the way you meet, greet, and treat everyone around you

(including those who've treated you in ways other than how you
deserve to be treated).

Are you aware that you have these choices?

Because you do.

❤

Say *yes* to your choices.

Scream *yes* to your choices.

For these are the choices that can take you in the direction that you
wish to go—

toward physical and emotional health, abundance,

happiness, peace, and positivity.

CHAPTER
30

Fill 'Er Up?
No Thanks!

I can think of a lot of things that need filling up at one time or another. Some of those things include: a bank account, a gas tank, a martini glass. Do you know what definitely *doesn't* need filling? Somebody else's shoes.

Call it anthropological curiosity. Call it abject boredom. Whatever the reason, a few years ago, I found myself watching a "How in the hell did *this* ever become popular" television show, wherein the object of this long-running program is to meet someone, ostensibly fall in love, and commit to a lifetime of marriage; all within a time span of an eight- to ten-week television season. This is preceded by participating in ridiculous "challenges" and competitions (presumably to impress the person doing the choosing), and thereafter behaving in what can only be described as a highly inappropriate manner with at least a dozen other people while on national television. I am clearly not a fan.[1]

However, while watching on this particular evening, my heart did go out to a young man on the show who had decided to venture back into the world of possibilities after losing his wife at a heartbreakingly young age. The young lady for whose affection the gentleman was competing[2] listened to the tragic story of the death of his bride and in response looked balefully at him, let out a sigh, and ruefully, if not-so-sympathetically groaned, "Boy, I would have some big shoes to fill."

(Now *there's* a way to let someone know how sorry you are for their loss: think about and actually voice how his painfully tragic situation affects *you.*)

It was mere moments later that this same young man who had courageously stepped out in faith and back into the dating world was unceremoniously booted off the show.[3]

Fast-forward to the young man being whisked away in a car, a dejected look on his face, wondering aloud why he had even bothered trying to find love again. My immediate concern was that he would take the aforementioned young lady at her word (because after all, who *is* going to fill his late wife's shoes?) and retreat to a place of raw grief and mourning. I was afraid that he would genuinely that there will be no love or happiness in his future, all because one unintentionally insensitive person felt that they couldn't "fill the shoes" of a late spouse.

---

1 Nor am I a prude. But come *on* . . .

2 Yes . . . *competing* for affection is apparently a thing.

3 While they may refer to the boot-off as a "ceremony," in point of fact, it is nothing more than public humiliation set to contrived, apocalyptic, horror-movie-reject music and referred to as "entertainment."

I grant you that I would not have recommended going on a nationally televised show as a first (or second or tenth) foray back into the World of Dating and Love. However, the potential for souring on living and loving post-loss, and the message that this particular show sent made me ask myself: *What about filling those shoes?*

When I made the decision to begin dating after my husband's death, at no time did I pull out any figurative shoes for anyone else to try and fill. Why? *People are not replaceable.*

I certainly would not want to be compared to anyone else. I wouldn't want someone to open a fashion magazine, point out an exquisitely tall, willowy brunette, and ask, "Why can't you be like her?" Unlike our young lady on the television show, I would also *never* look at someone and remark about how *I* would have big shoes to fill because, in contrast to what was being said on the television show, the *actual* reality (as opposed to *television* reality) is that people are not replaceable. The very expression, "filling shoes," is a poorly disguised way of either making comparisons to or outright expecting someone new to be exactly like a predecessor. It's patently unfair to draw any comparisons between a late spouse or partner and anyone who is currently or may become a part of your life. It is for this reason that I was never interested in attempting to fill my late husband's shoes.

I was blessed to have found love with a man who never once expected me to replace or fill the shoes of anyone who came before me, nor did he once try to replace or fill the shoes of anyone who was a part of my previous life. Dave came complete with his own fabulous shoes, if you will, and expected the same of me. Neither one of us is now or was ever expected to allegorically put on and clomp around in anyone else's ill-fitting, not-quite-right shoes in an attempt to become a carbon copy of someone else, because—repeat after me—people are not replaceable.

Whether you unreasonably expect it of yourself or you expect it of another, attempting to replace a person who is no longer here is essentially holding up an invisible and unrealistic "yardstick" to the dearly departed, an unfair exercise at best. Companionship and love are not about any kind of competition. Companionship and love are not comparison-shopping, and they are certainly not about metaphorical shoe-filling. Instead, revel in the uniqueness that is you, as well as the person or people whom you welcome into your life, now and going forward. The only shoes that you should ever be interested in filling . . . are your own.

EKITA!

Our hearts have an infinite capacity to love.

It's a fact.

No matter what new love comes into your life

or in what form that new love arrives

(because new love doesn't necessarily have to be a person),

your heart can love to the extent that you permit it to do so.

❤

And if it's your choice to love something or someone new,

you should permit your heart to do so without any limitations.

None.

❤

Your heart has broken.

Your heart has wept.

Your heart works overtime every single day

in order to mend.

Why not allow your heart every opportunity to soar . . .

to sing . . .

to dance . . .

to delight in life once again?

❤

No guilt,
no "cheating"
and no "forgetting" the past
is or should ever be involved in loving anything or anyone
in a new life.
Don't allow anyone to try to convince you otherwise
. . . including you.

Is There
Really Love After Loss?
The Answer Is . . .

An incredibly loaded question and phrased in so many different ways, "Is there *really* love after loss?" is echoed by most in the widowed community, and it elicits a variety of responses. There are widowed who vow never to permit their hearts to so much as lean in the direction of romantic love ever again. There are others who are quite open to the prospect of loving once again. Still others choose to remain on their own and are happily satisfied in that choice. However, I have found that those who question the existence of love after loss are really asking, "Is it *okay* for me to love after my loss?"

Too often, and unfortunately, the widowed will answer that question for themselves based on one of two misguided factors: the negative influence of those around them (i.e., the "Once Widowed,

Always Widowed" Gang) or succumbing to the overwhelming guilt that can accompany that question. We'll explore the matter of what is okay or appropriate post-loss shortly. Meanwhile, I'm hoping that at this point, you have renewed hope for your future and have begun learning how to design that future. In so doing, I also hope that you'll choose to stop listening to that which is detrimental to your healing journey and contradictory to what your own heart is telling you to do.

So, let's have a closer look at entertaining the thought of seeking companionship and love as a widowed person.

Giving Up Before You Even Begin

Whenever I hear a widowed say that they've given up on any prospect for new love (for whatever reason), it hurts my heart, mostly because what I hear them saying is that they are dishonoring something that they really want to do and have instead chosen to give up on the life that they wish to design. However, when I hear this sentiment coming from either a guilt-based place or from listening to seriously poor advice (or both), I really want to just scream very loudly (something at which I excel).

I understand throwing one's hands up in the air after a lousy date and declaring early retirement from romantic pursuits. Hell, I understand it after a hundred lousy dates. However, to unilaterally decide that you will never love again because you are either being improperly influenced or you feel some semblance of guilt is just wrong.

The "Cheating Twinges"

Several months after Mike's death, I needed medical attention. Between the fact that I was a new widow and that I needed medical attention, I was completely unconcerned with my appearance (as are most of us when we're ill). Dressed in a manner that could only be described as slapdash (and that's being diplomatic), my hair was carelessly slung into a ponytail, my face was devoid of makeup, and my "couture" of the day consisted of a ragged, baggy sweat suit. I was waiting in the examining room when in walked the doctor, whom I had never before met. He. Was. *Gorgeous.*

For the first time in too long to remember, I was acutely aware of my appearance (or the distinct lack thereof). Worse, I was so disconcerted by these sudden feelings of attraction to a man other than my late husband, I didn't know what to do with myself. I felt as though I were cheating on Mike, our marriage, our child, his memory, and pretty much everyone I ever knew.

After I left the doctor's office, I immediately called my rabbi (from the parking lot of the doctor's office) and demanded to know what was *wrong* with me. My husband was gone for a few months and here I am, worried about what I look like and finding men attractive. What in hell is the matter with me? Imagine my total shock when I was told that absolutely *nothing* was wrong with me.

Remember what you learned earlier in Chapter Twenty-Six ("Loyalty Versus Living Again . . ."). Even if not the exact words, the sentiment in your wedding vows was to the effect of, "Until death do us part." You upheld your end of the vows, as did your beloved. In short, there is no "cheating" going on. Should the time come that you feel ready to at least entertain thoughts of companionship, there is absolutely no reason to feel any guilt whatsoever. Whether you are beating yourself up with guilt or you are allowing others to do it to you, you must commit to ridding yourself of any guilt that you may be feeling in tandem with moving forward into a new life—one that may include companionship and/or love in it.

There Is Neither Present nor Future Without the Past

There are people who (supposedly) fall in love with a widowed and thereafter either expect or outright demand that the widowed both emotionally and practically disconnect from and eradicate the past that they lived with their late spouse—and they are expected to do so with the apparent ease of erasing a whiteboard. More often than not, the reason for this attitude can be boiled down to one issue: insecurity.

Widowed who feel compelled to put their past on an invisible shelf have had the sad misfortune of involving themselves with those who refuse to accept them for who and what they are, past and all. When you stop and think that the very word "widowed" automatically lets society at large know who you are and that which you have endured, it doesn't make a lot of sense.

To put it in ass-kicking, Boot-Camp-blunt terms, those who are threatened by someone else's past (*whatever* that past entails) are insecure, immature, and woefully insensitive. These are the same people who don't believe that men and women are capable of being the best of friends and nothing more. These are the same people who demand to be joined at the hip with their significant others. These are people who go through one another's cell phones searching desperately for something covert. It is insecurity of the highest order... and it is *not* okay.

Are there men and women out there who simply don't want to deal with the widowed person and the past life that automatically accompanies them? Of course there are. I also recognize how fortunate I am to have found someone who both had and has no problem with my widowhood (and no, he is not a widower). However, what you may not realize is that between the time I began dating (which was approximately two years after Mike's death) and the time that I initially met Dave, I endured five not-always-fun-filled years of dating a wide variety of men, very few of whom cared to deal with the fact that I was (a) widowed and (b) writing for and working within the bereaved community.

It is certainly a prerogative to choose not to date someone who is widowed (or someone who is divorced or someone who has children or someone who is tall or short or skinny or not). What is *not* a prerogative is dating someone with the full knowledge of who and what they are—and subsequently expecting or demanding that they change. To be expected to essentially "erase" your past, be it by disposal of photographs, mementos, and the like, or the disposal of traditions or comfort measures (paying a visit to a gravesite, remembrances at the holidays, or on angelversaries, etc.), is at best unreasonable and at worst unconscionable.

Further, let's not forget one other very common and important component of widowhood: children. Are our children also expected to forget their absent parent in favor of a new love because the new love feels somehow threatened? Are you *kidding*? How do we teach our children that the heart expands infinitely to embrace any love we wish to include in our lives if they are being taught that by loving someone new, we must immediately eliminate the "late"? This is not a closet cleanout to make room for new clothes. To treat a late spouse and/or late parent in this fashion is not just morally wrong, it can be extremely damaging in terms of grief recovery.

Anyone who has an issue because of how you choose to remember, love, and honor the past without living in it is not taking you in the direction that you wish to go. Anyone who is modeling behavior that is striking a negative undertone is not taking you in the direction that you wish to go. Anyone who makes demands that are negative and counterintuitive (insisting on the ridding of mementos and photographs; insisting on dispensing with traditions that were obviously of consolation, etc.) *is not taking you in the direction that you wish to go.*

Following is an absolutely wonderful observation made by a widower who wrote to me several years ago. His outlook and attitude are both an inspiration and contagious (and if not literally contagious, it certainly ought to be).

"I became a widower twenty-one years ago, when I lost my wife and nearly lost my four young children in an auto accident. I remarried years later to an incredibly wonderful woman. But there isn't a day that goes by that I don't think of my first wife, miss her terribly, and still love her unconditionally. Thank God for my second wife [for understanding] and not being threatened by my love for my first wife. Anyone who 'understands, and gives you grief about that isn't worth a tinker's damn!"

To him and to all of you, I simply say: Amen.

The Key Word in "New Beginnings" Is *New*

All of that said, the widowed, too, bear responsibility within a new relationship. Examine yourself honestly:

- ✓ Are you building shrines in your home to your late beloved? I am not speaking of a couple of pictures or a small grouping of mementos; I'm talking about full-out shrines (and I've seen them).
- ✓ Are you constantly dwelling on your previous life? Worse, are you making comparisons (out loud or silently) between a prospective new love and your late beloved? This is completely and totally unfair to *any* new person in your life.
- ✓ Are you unwilling to accept that previous and future lives can be successfully integrated?

Remember the discussion in Chapter Thirty ("Fill 'Er Up? No Thanks!"). You cannot use your late beloved or the life you lived with them as that metaphorical yardstick against which you measure everyone else. You can't begin sentences with, "Joe always used to . . ." or, "Jane would have never . . .," because absolutely no one "always" did something right or "never" did anything wrong. Everyone deserves to be judged on their own merits and should not be compared to *anyone* in your past. You are making a new beginning, and the most important word in that sentence to remember is *new*.

The Reality of Remarriage After Widowhood

A few years ago, a well-known and much respected actor once mentioned in an interview that he still thinks about his late wife. People were shocked at this supposedly "stunning revelation," as the same actor has been happily remarried for many years. This sort of shocked reaction begs an obvious question. Since when did remarriage become an equation that reads: "Remarried equals Forgetting"?

This latest in a long line of widowed-myths implies that once remarried, the life previously lived somehow fades into oblivion all because the widowed has found a new life with new love in it. Because of this new life, the remarried widowed is apparently never again sad or wistful because their late beloved is no longer here.

Conversely and equally perplexing is the companion myth, "Once Widowed, Always Widowed," wherein the widowed should assume an attitude that they have "caught their limit"; that once their beloved has passed away, a widowed's destiny is to remain forlornly alone and longing for a life that is no longer here to live. A widowed should thereafter resign themselves to functioning in life with grief and mourning as their core and living a destiny that they did not choose.

The reality of spousal loss that is so important for both the widowed and those who surround them to understand is that (repeat EKITA alert):[1]

You can honor your past,

you can treasure your past,

you can and you should love your past . . .

you do not have to *live* in your past.

When it comes to love, our hearts are truly without capacity or limits. If this were not the case, we would each have only one

---

1 The most important advice bears repeating. I believe this to be among the most important words that I've ever written.

child, because how could our hearts *possibly* expand to love more than one? We all have an infinite capacity to love, and should that be a widowed's choice, finding love in a new life can and should absolutely be part of their dynamic. Love for a new person is not mutually exclusive of love for others in your life. Loving again does not mean that the love for a late beloved goes away. It doesn't. Furthermore, loving again does not dishonor or disrespect the person who is no longer here, nor does it disrespect the *memory* of that person. This is a concept that can create a fair amount of discord (especially within families) when a widowed finds companionship or love once again.

We discussed the concept of grief shaming in Chapter Twenty-One ("Grief Shaming: The Latest Form of Bereavement Judgment"). Rarely does grief shaming rear its ugly head faster than when a widowed announces that they have again fallen in love and—*gasp!*—their intent to remarry. Actor and comedian Patton Oswalt joined the "club that nobody wants to join" when he suddenly lost his beloved wife, journalist, and true crime writer Michelle McNamara. As is generally the case, sympathy poured in and compassionate sentiment for the much-admired actor (now a widower with a young daughter) was swift and sweet . . . until just over a year later, when he had the temerity to announce that he'd found love once again and was engaged to be married.

The tenor of public support quickly turned venomous. Disapproval and the harshest of judgment rained down upon a man who had done nothing more than move forward with his life, but had the nerve to do so without taking the temperature of the public.[2] I was devastated at the commentary to which so many other people felt that they had a right. Who among us has the right to judge another person or cast aspersion upon how someone chooses to conduct their life, particularly when it comes to something as intensely personal as deciding to get married?

Imagine my delight when I was approached by *The Canadian Press*[3] to offer commentary on Mr. Oswalt's engagement announcement and the overwhelmingly negative response. Permit me to share a slice of I'm Really Cranky Pie with you:

> "People are quick to bifurcate life and love into an either-or proposition. You either love your past and the person you lost and get [into] this once-a-widow, always-a-widow head space and stay there, or you can recognize that the heart expands infinitely to embrace all of the love that it wants to. This is a new life that [Oswalt's] in now and he's entitled to a new love in his new life. Nobody can dictate that, and I'm appalled that anybody, especially someone who hides anonymously behind a keyboard and screen, feels that they have that right. You cannot live your life by opinion poll.

Told you I was cranky—though admittedly, my crankiness was laughingly assuaged when I later read that Mr. Oswalt referred to the anonymous commenting trolls as "bitter grub worms."

People who surround the remarried or re-partnered widowed can also interpret newfound love and happiness as not grieving "right," not having experienced grief at all, completely "forgetting"

---

2 A public that, I might add, were not members of the widowed community, very few of whom would ever deign to behave in such a hideous manner.

3 Excerpt: "No 'Right' Timeline for Romance After Death of Spouse: Experts," by Sheryl Ubelacker, *The Canadian Press*, July 13, 2017.

the past (as if *that* is even possible), or believing that we have collectively dusted off our hands and are glancing around as if to say, "Okay, that's done and over with . . . who's next?" The fact is that even in a wonderful new life, things like holidays, birthdays, anniversaries, "angelversaries," and children realizing various life milestones can all serve as painful reminders that someone who a widowed loves without measure is no longer here to celebrate, witness, and in general, be a part of a life that was built with love.

Years after losing my late husband, I can tell you without reservation that I still love him and I still treasure the life we had together. However, both Kendall and I have also moved forward into a beautiful new life. Eleven years old when her daddy passed away, Kendall is now a lovely young woman who enjoys a thriving career and is building a life of her own with the love of *her* life. Dave and I have created a lovely blended family, augmented by two more daughters. To top it all off, I have the privilege of being on a mission of service and support to others in need.

Now, by living this new life, does that mean that I have forgotten about or betrayed my past life? Absolutely not. Does it mean that after Mike died, I should have stayed inside the house in my pajamas and kept the blinds closed forever? What would *that* have accomplished? I chose instead to grieve in my way and in my time, help Kendall with and through her own grief recovery, and slowly, yet steadily, move into a life of my own design—a design that happily included new love and new adventures to go along with that new love.

The love that you have for your late beloved will never go away. Not ever. Not with the passage of time. Not with the introduction of a new person into your life and into your heart. Not with the eight jillion people around you saying things like, "Well, you should be over it by now." I am honoring Mike's legacies of love and service by continuing to move forward, by modeling the best examples that I can for my daughters, by serving a community that I love, and by nurturing a family whom I love beyond words. By doing all of these things, I am indeed honoring the legacies of love and service that Mike left to us to carry forward.

You can do the same—if and when you choose to do so. Remarriage does *not* equal forgetting; let no one tell you otherwise.

So, *is* there really love after loss? The answer is . . . entirely up to *you*. There absolutely can be love after loss if you choose to seek it. However, I am quick to reiterate that there is nothing wrong whatsoever with *choosing* (note the emphasis, please) to remain on your own and loving that choice as well.

It is vital that you thoroughly understand that loving again does *not* imply lack of or the end of love for the past, and the person or people with whom you shared that past. You are *not* destined to remain in mourning forever—that is not why you are here. Embrace and carry forward the legacies that were entrusted to you by your late beloved. If you choose it, living your new life can include companionship *and* love. Choose carefully, choose wisely . . . and love again abundantly.

EKITA!

No one likes being widowed, nor is the widowhood

journey something that

anyone would intentionally seek out.

No one likes the word *widowed* very much either.

However, remember that the word widowed is also a badge of honor.

How?

Think about it.

❤

Regardless of the length of your marriage,

your engagement, or your relationship,

you were together *forever*, even if forever was not very long for you.

How many people can say the same in this day and age?

❤

You have also survived one of the most horrible

experiences that you'll ever know.

Within that survival, you have discovered strength

that many will not realize—

even in what feels like your weakest moments.

You have also discovered your resilience, perseverance,

determination, and the true depth of your spirit.

❤

So wear the badge

and be proud.

Be proud that you were together forever.

Be proud that you fulfilled vows and promises

until death did you part.

Be proud of the legacies of love that have been entrusted to you

by someone who loved you just as much as you loved them.

Be proud of how far you've come on your healing journey . . .

even if that journey began a very short time ago.

Be proud of who you are today, right this minute . . .

because you should be.

Epilogue

A s you continue your healing journey, it's vital that you keep the word "ownership" in the front of your mind. The rightful ownership of your journey must remain with *you*. Therefore, to serve as an important reminder of that ownership, in order that you will never again need to ask any question beginning with the words, "Is it okay if I . . .?" (sometimes disguised as "When is it appropriate to . . .?"), and realizing that sometimes all we need is for just one person who has walked a similar path to quietly and gently say, "It really *is* okay." The following is a partial list of what it is absolutely, positively okay for you to do after becoming widowed:

It's okay to smile.

It's okay to laugh.

It's okay to laugh really hard.

It's okay to cry.

It's okay if your children see you cry.

It's okay to feel weak.

It's okay to feel angry.

It's okay to say, "I need help."

It's okay to feel relief.

It's okay to feel peace.

It's okay to travel places, be they new and exciting or comfortably familiar.

It's okay to be content at home.

It's okay to pay attention to yourself and your needs without feeling guilty.

It's okay to socialize.

It's okay to say, "Perhaps another time."

It's okay to try new things.

It's okay to rest securely in the comfort of daily routine.

It's okay to remain in the home where you shared a life and created memories.

It's okay to move into a new home and create new memories.

It's okay to continue wearing your engagement and/or your wedding rings.

It's okay to wear your rings on your right hand.

It's okay to take your rings off.

It's okay to create a new piece of jewelry from your rings and wear it proudly.

It's okay to say, "Yes."

It's okay to say, "No."

It's okay to honor traditions in memory of your beloved.

It's okay to mix it up a bit, whatever your "it" may be.

It's okay to display selected mementos of your previous life.

It's okay to store mementos as heirlooms for loved ones or future generations.

It's okay to seek companionship again.

It's okay to fall in love again.

It's okay to fall back out of love, yet continue to seek it.

It's okay to choose to be on your own and cherish every single minute of it.

It's okay to forever love your past life and the person with whom you shared it.

It's okay to find "forever" with another, to whom you will refer as the love of your new life.

It's okay to move happily forward into that life and the new experiences and memories that it will bring you.

It will *always* and *forever* be okay to *live*.

It really *is* okay. It really is *going* to be okay.
And so will you.

Recommended Resources

I strongly encourage you to continue your healing journey by visiting the following organizations. Note that all of them can also be located via Facebook, Twitter, and various other social media platforms.

Crisis Intervention and Programs

1. **National Suicide Prevention Lifeline:** *www.suicidepreventionlife line.org.* (800) 273-8255. Help is available by telephone twenty-four hours a day, seven days a week.

2. **Alcoholics Anonymous:** *www.aa.org.* A comprehensive website providing information as to local AA resources in the United States and Canada, daily reflections, and an online bookstore.

3. **Narcotics Anonymous:** *www.na.org.* Based upon the same principles as AA, their website also offers assistance in locating local resources, as well as an online magazine.

4. **National Eating Disorders Association:** *www.nationaleatingdis orders.org.* (800) 931-2237. Their website also includes live chat, a blog, and member forums; encompassing all eating disorders in the spectrum.

5. **Debtors Anonymous (compulsive shopping/spending):** *www .debtorsanonymous.org.* The website includes a "Getting Started" tab, which will direct you to free literature, FAQ, and other helpful information, as well as assist you in locating a meeting near you.

6. **Sexual Compulsives Anonymous (SCA):** *www.sca-recovery.org*. The website serves the United States, Canada, and several other countries. There is also guidance as to locating meetings and an online newsletter.

Serving the Widowed Community

Facebook page, "Carole Brody Fleet": Includes "hot-topic" discussions, inspirational thoughts, and other information for the widowed community.

Facebook page, "WWS Peer-Led Support Forum": A Facebook page for widows only, this is a closed group where discussions take place that can be seen only by other members of the closed community. Send a request to the administrator of the page to be added, and please ensure that your Facebook profile can be verified.

The American Widow Project at *www.americanwidowproject.org*: An award-winning nonprofit that provides resources, products, services, and special outings and gatherings for widows and families of military personnel.

TAPS (Tragedy Assistance Program for Survivors): *www.taps.org*. Since 1994, TAPS has assisted surviving families, casualty officers, and caregivers, providing compassionate care to all those grieving the loss of a loved one in the military. TAPS provides 24/7 comfort through a national peer support network and connection to grief resources, all at no cost to surviving families and loved ones.

Soaring Spirits Loss Foundation: *www.sslf.org*. An award-winning nonprofit organization that operates several programs for the widowed community, including the annual Camp Widow International Conferences *(www.campwidow.org)*.

The Liz Logelin Foundation: *www.TheLizLogelinFoundation.org*. Awards monetary grants to meet qualifying widowed families' emotional and short-term financial needs.

Social Security Administration: *www.ssa.gov.* Provides specific instructions and directions on obtaining survivor benefits for the widowed and for their children and also provides information on various programs and assistance available to survivors and their families.

Department of Veterans Affairs: *www.va.gov.* Provides specific instructions and directions on obtaining benefits for survivors of military personnel (active, inactive, retired, or deceased) and also provides information on various programs and assistance available to survivors and their families.

About the Author

Widely recognized as America's go-to expert on life adversity and grief recovery, Carole Brody Fleet is also a three-time contributor to the iconic Chicken Soup for the Soul book series and a previous top contributor to the *Huffington Post* and *ThirdAge.com*. Ms. Fleet has appeared on *Good Morning America, The CBS Evening News*, and numerous television and syndicated radio shows throughout the United States, Canada, and the United Kingdom. She has appeared in *USA Today, The New York Times*, the *Chicago Tribune, U.S. News and World Report, Woman's World, Psychology Today, Health*, and hundreds of other publications and websites worldwide.

Ms. Fleet speaks internationally to: business and networking organizations; corporations; social and charitable/non-profit organizations; students; military organizations; women's conferences and organizations; the healthcare, hospice/palliative and bereavement industries; and organizations serving those who have been touched by the pain and challenge of loss.

Other books by Carole Brody Fleet include: the #1 release *When Bad Things Happen to Good Women; Happily EVEN After*, winner of the prestigious Books for a Better Life Award; and the critically praised national bestseller *Widows Wear Stilettos*.

For additional information, please visit www.WidowsWear Stilettos.com, *www.CaroleFleetSpeaker.com*, and on Facebook at Carole Brody Fleet.